rHODODENDRONS

a care manual

Kenneth Cox

LAUREL GLEN PUBLISHING

First published in the United States
in 1998 by Laurel Glen Publishing
5880 Oberlin Drive, Suite 400
San Diego, CA 92121-9653
1-800-284-3580

First published in Great Britain
in 1998 by Hamlyn,
an imprint of Reed Consumer
Books Limited
Michelin House, 81 Fulham Road,
London SW3 6RB
and Auckland, Melbourne,
Singapore, and Toronto

ISBN 1-57145-620-1

1 2 3 4 5 98 99 00 01 02

Produced by Toppan
Printed in China

Publishing Director
Laura Bamford
Creative Director
Keith Martin
Executive Editor
Julian Brown
Executive Art Editor
Mark Winwood
Assistant Editor
Karen O'Grady
Designer
Ruth Hope
Production Controller
Julie Hadingham
Picture Researcher
Liz Fowler
Photography
Peter Myers
and Shaun Myers

Library of Congress
Cataloging-in-Publication Data

Cox, Kenneth N. E.
(Kenneth Nicolas Evan), 1964-
Rhododendrons :
a care manual / Kenneth Cox.
p. cm.
Includes bibliographical
references and index.
ISBN 1-57145-620-1
1. Rhododendrons. I. Title.
SB413.R47C6235 1998
635.9'3366--dc 21   98-18555
CIP

Contents

Introduction

The word "rhododendron" means different things to different people. Perhaps most familiar to inhabitants of the U.K. are the grand country houses with driveways lined with large old pink and purple flowered hybrid rhododendrons in late spring. In areas of Britain with a high rainfall in the south and west of the country, the word rhododendron produces the reaction "weed" and "pest"; here, getting rid of the invasive *Rhododendron ponticum* is a common task.

In North America, on both the West and East Coasts, wild rhododendrons and azaleas are found in forests and on mountains, as they are in the Alps of Europe. In Nepal and Tibet, the dried leaves of alpine varieties are used for incense in Buddhist temples. To the style gurus of gardening, rhododendrons are often frowned upon as an unfashionable plant, though of course they are planted and enjoyed by millions in gardens all over the world. And yet I am sure that a quick glance through the photographs in this book will reveal some surprises.

The genus *Rhododendron* includes an astounding variety of plant types with a range of flower shapes and colors that are second to none in the plant world. One of the things this book aims to do is to debunk the stereotypes associated with this enormous, astonishingly varied genus and, hopefully, to provide new ideas for enhancing the landscape with imaginative uses of this king of plants.

Rhododendrons come in all shapes and sizes and the genus includes all of the azaleas. Perhaps most familiar are the large, blowsy hybrids, which are widely planted around country houses and stately homes. In fact, these hardy hybrids form only a small proportion of the total picture. Many rhododendron species and hybrids have tiny leaves and grow only a few inches high. At the other end of the scale there are giants with leaves up to 3 feet (1m) in length. Another part of the genus encompasses the tropical Vireya rhododendrons found in Indonesia and neighboring areas. These need to be kept in greenhouses in all but the mildest climates.

My family has been long associated with rhododendron collecting and growing. My grandfather, Euan Cox, had his interest sparked off when he was invited to accompany the well-known plant hunter Reginald Farrer to Burma in 1919. Knowing virtually nothing about plants before he went on this expedition, he returned with considerable knowledge and spent the rest of his life in gardening-related activities. He edited horticultural publications, wrote gardening columns and books on plants and gardening, in the process enthusing my father, with whom he started a rhododendron nursery at Glendoick. My father, Peter Cox, V.M.H., is himself a nurseryman, plant-hunter, author, and rhododendron hybridizer, and I suppose it was inevitable that I would follow in his footsteps.

Kenneth Cox

Where Do Rhododendrons Come From?

Rhododendrons belong to the family Ericaceae, which also includes the heathers, *Kalmia, Enkianthus, Gaultheria*, blueberries, and cranberries. What most of these plants have in common is their requirement for acid soil and a fair amount of moisture. Rhododendrons are found throughout much of the northern hemisphere and their distribution extends into the southern hemisphere through the Malay peninsula and the Indonesian islands, with a single species (some authorities claim two) on a mountain in northern Australia. The distribution of temperate rhododendrons, the kind commonly grown as garden plants in parts of the world with cold winters, centers on China and the Himalayas. There are several species native to Europe, while most of the deciduous azalea species come from North America. There are no species native to South America or Africa. The European species, such as the alpine *R. ferrugineum* and the sweetly scented pontic azalea *R. luteum*, have long been cultivated as garden plants and are referred to in both horticultural and medicinal literature of the sixteenth and seventeenth centuries. It was not until the introduction of species of azalea from America to Europe in the seventeenth and eighteenth century that rhododendrons began to be quite widely grown as garden plants. By 1800 there were around 12 species in cultivation in Europe, including the infamous *R. ponticum*. It was not long before hybridizers got to work on the raw

Right: Snow beds at 13,000 ft. (4000m) in the Th'Lonok valley, Sikkim, with rhododendrons in blossom (Kinchin-Junga in the distance) from Sir Joseph Hooker's journal.

Below: Joseph Hooker collecting plants for Kew Gardens in the Sikkim Himalaya, by Frank Stone, A.R.A.

material, trying to improve on nature. From 1810–1840 a range of hardy azalea hybrids known as the Ghents were developed, as well as the first so-called hardy hybrids such as "Cunningham's White," raised at a nursery in Edinburgh and still one of the most popular hybrids today.

The next great breakthrough was the discovery and introduction of the first Himalayan rhododendrons. Joseph Hooker's expedition to Sikkim in 1850 collected 45 species, most newly described. Many of these were soon recognized for their garden value and were in turn

used to breed a huge range of hybrids. The Himalayan species included the blood-red *R. thomsonii* with rounded leaves and fine peeling bark, the tall and vigorous *R. griffithianum* with massive white flowers, and the magnificent *R. falconeri* with large furry leaves and enormous trusses of creamy flowers. Suddenly, rhododendron species and hybrids were everywhere. No self-respecting country house was complete without beds of them incorporated into park landscapes. At the same time, and coinciding with the vogue for hothouses, tropical species were introduced and many hybrids were raised. Alas, unlike their cold-hardy

Tab.I.

relatives, the tropical rhododendrons mostly met a sad end as heating was shut off during wartime, and the great Victorian conservatories were abandoned. Recent years have seen a huge resurgence of interest in these tropical or Vireya rhododendrons, particularly in areas such as California, New Zealand, and southeastern Australia, where they can be grown outdoors.

The beginning of the twentieth century saw the introduction of evergreen azaleas from Japan to Europe and America and, more significantly, the opening up of China to foreign exploration. Following in the footsteps of French missionaries turned botanists, Ernest Wilson's first expedition to Hupeh province in 1899 introduced *R. auriculatum, R. maculiferum,* and *R. sutchuenense.* He returned to China in 1903–4 and was followed by George Forrest in Yunnan in 1904, Frank Kingdon Ward in 1911, and Joseph Rock in 1920. These plant hunters sent back specimens and seeds of thousands of species of plants, including several hundred rhododendrons, which were duly described in herbaria at the British Museum or at botanic gardens such as the Arnold Arboretum, Edinburgh or Kew Gardens, London. Gardeners in Europe, the United States and elsewhere grew the seeds on a huge scale. This was the era

of the woodland garden, and great gardens such as Caerhays and Exbury in the U.K. were laid out, with their owners competing for awards at the exclusive gentleman's club that was The Rhododendron Society.

Some of the recently introduced species such as

R. dalhousiae from the book Rhododendrons of the Sikkim Himalaya by Walter Fitch from field drawings in William Hooker's journal, circa 1850.

R. griersonianum and *R. wardii* soon proved to be excellent parents and many new hybrids of all shapes and sizes were produced. A number of the hybrids listed in the Plant Directory section, such as "Loderi," "Fabia," "Vanessa," and "Lady Chamberlain" were raised at this time. The introduction of *R. yakushimanum,* a

compact, hardy, easily grown species from Japan, in the early 1930s, proved to be another important breakthrough. This species became the most popular hybridizing parent of all time, with many breeders in the U.K., Germany, and North America (and elsewhere) raising "yak"

12

hybrids, a range of low-growing, compact and hardy plants with showy flowers of many different shades. At Glendoick, Peter Cox began hybridizing very dwarf varieties in the late 1950s and selections from this breeding program, which continues today, are the well-known bird hybrids such as "Curlew" and "Ptarmigan." China, and many of the other countries in the area, closed their doors to foreigners during the 1950s, '60s, and '70s. Only a handful of new rhododendron species

were introduced during this period. These included my parents' discovery *R. coxianum* from N.E. India, the wonderful *R. pachysanthum* from Taiwan, and several species of Vireyas from Borneo and New Guinea.

China reopened its borders in 1981 and my father, Peter Cox, who had waited 30 years for the chance, was on the first major expedition back into the stomping ground of his heroes from the early part of the century. The Sino-British Expedition to the Cangshan (in Yunnan) was the first of many which have explored and reexplored this extraordinarily plant-rich region of

A magnificent mountain view in Pome, southeastern Tibet, taken on one of the author's expeditions, with the yellow *R. wardii* and the pinkish-purple *R. calostrotum.*

the world. Since 1981, many new plant species have been introduced, including several new species of rhododendron. Among the most important of these in the last few years are the giant *R. sinofalconeri* with yellow flowers and large leaves, the red species from the Yunnan/Sichuan border *R. ochraceum,* and the neat, deep pink, dwarf species *R. dendrocharis.*

I have led several expeditions to southeastern Tibet during the last few years. We have managed to explore farther than our predecessors and to introduce several species such as *R. bulu* and *R. dignabile* for the first time. "Surely there aren't any more new

species out there," people often say to me. In fact these are being named all the time and there are several desirable species which we know only from photographs. Recent expeditions to Vietnam have revealed a wealth of interesting new species which should make fine garden plants in mild climates. There are still areas that have never been explored properly and there are certain to be more good plants out there about which we know nothing.

Rhododendrons in the Wild

There are few, if any, writers in the field of plant exploration to rival the plant hunter and prolific author, Frank Kingdon Ward. Here he describes the "rhododendron fairyland" of the Doshong La in southeastern Tibet in his book *Riddle of the Tsangpo Gorges*:

"The Valley, flanked by gray cliffs, roofed by gray skies, with the white snowfields above, spouting water which splashed and gurgled in a dozen babbling becks; and everywhere the rocks swamped under a tidal wave of intense colors which gleam and glow in leagues of breaking light. The colors leap at you as you climb the moraine: Scarlet Runner dripping in blood red rivers from the ledges, choppy sulphur seas breaking from a long, low surf of pink."

Few sights in the world can equal these plants in full flower in their native mountains. The greatest concentration of rhododendron species (around 300–400) is found in an area from Nepal, Bhutan and Burma, north and east through southeastern Tibet into Yunnan and Sichuan provinces in China. Here the mighty rivers, the Tsangpo, the Salween, the Mekong, and the Yangtze flow through deep gorges at altitudes of up to 9,000–10,000 ft. (2,700–3000m) while on either side, mountain ranges climb to 25,000 ft. (7500m) or more. Wherever the rainfall is high enough for rich forest, there are usually rhododendrons growing from around the level of the river up to 16,000 ft. (4900m) or so. At the lower altitudes in deep, lush forest, epiphytic species can be found (which grow on other plants or mossy logs) and large-leaved species, such as the magnificent *R. sinogrande*, with leaves up to 3 feet (1m) in length. A little higher up, rhododendrons often form the dominant forest: in Nepal the red *R. arboreum* paints the hillsides a dazzling shade in March and April.

Elsewhere, species such as *R. phaeochrysum*, *R. oreotrephes*, and *R. uvariifolium* form a dense understory under the *Picea* and *Abies*, such that whole hillsides can burst into flower. A little higher still and the trees start to thin. Here shrubby species such as *R. campylocarpum* or *R. roxieanum* may be the dominant vegetation at and above the treeline. Nearer the top, the leaves get smaller and the species become lower growing. Here on the windswept moorland you might find Frank Kingdon Ward's "Scarlet Runner," *R. forrestii*, with its bright red waxy flowers often opening up soon after the leaves emerge from the melting snow, or one of the small blue-purple Lapponica species such as *R. fastigiatum*. It is possible to find 20–30 species on a single mountainside in some of the richer areas, and the rhododendrons are usually accompanied by *Primula*, *Meconopsis*, *Diapensia*, *Clematis*, *Deutzia*, *Sorbus*, orchids and many other of our most common garden plants.

If the flowers were not enough, the rhododendrons grow in some of the world's most dramatic scenery. Forget any photographs you have seen. Nothing prepares you for the vastness of the Himalayan and Chinese mountains until you are looking at 10–13,000 ft. (3–4,000m) of mountain towering above you when you are actually already standing at 10,000 ft. (3,000m) yourself. Short of breath but triumphant, you can sit at the top of a mountain pass, surrounded by snow-covered peaks, with the largest natural flower gardens you will ever see spread out around you. It is not at all hard to become hooked on rhododendrons, faced with such a feast!

A forest of *Abies delavayi* and *R. selense* var. *jucundum* on the Cangshan, Yunnan, China, taken on one of the author's plant hunting exhibitions.

Site Preparation

Choosing a Site

Unless you are lucky enough to own a large estate, it is likely that you will have a limited number of possible sites in which to plant rhododendrons. Even within a small garden, however, aspect, wind shelter, shade, and frost drainage can vary considerably, so choosing the best site is important. Situations facing away from the sun are colder with less light and warmth to ripen wood, but the advantages are that the plants require less watering, and growth and flowering will come later, which is useful where spring frosts are a problem. In areas where hot summers cause high soil temperatures, such aspects may be the best option, both from a point of view of shade and keeping the soil temperature down. Strong winds can damage rhododendrons, especially those with large leaves, so it is important to be aware of the prevailing winds when selecting your planting sites. There are certain places where rhododendrons just will not grow. Alkaline soil, marshy and boggy ground with stagnant water, or directly under mature beech trees are three examples.

Left: Japanese maples (*Acer palmatum*) make an excellent foil for evergreen azaleas flowering in the woodland garden at Exbury Gardens, Hampshire, England, in May and June.

Right: The fine apricot-pink and salmon American hybrid "Virginia Richards" planted in a mixed border of perennials and rhododendrons.

Shade

The advantage of good shade-cover from trees or artificial materials is the protection it offers from frost (especially in spring when flowers and growth are vulnerable), sunburn, and heat. In very cold areas, such as northern Europe and northeastern North America, winter sun coupled with extreme cold can cause a great deal of damage, as the plant loses water to evaporation but cannot replace it because the ground is frozen. Shade can greatly reduce this risk. The disadvantages of shade can, however, be significant. Many shade trees are very demanding of moisture. Trees such as beech and sycamore are particularly greedy, and rhododendrons growing under or near such trees invariably suffer from drought. Oak, larch, pines, spruce, and fir are less greedy and let in more light. Heavy shade also causes spindly, straggly, and sparse plants which often flower poorly.

How much shade rhododendrons require depends on the varieties you grow and where you live. In northern climates such as Scotland and Scandinavia where summer sun is not all that intense, most varieties grow and flower best with no overhead shade. Look up from where a plant is and you should be able to see sky. As you move south, foliage sunburn, flowers quickly wilting and high soil temperatures are all factors which indicate need for greater shade. In eastern U.S.A. and other areas with high summer temperatures, most varieties require a considerable amount of shade to avoid damage.

As a general maxim, I would say that people tend to garden in too much shade. This may not be through choice; often there are restrictions and difficulties in felling trees. It is worth bearing in mind, however, that it is always easier to fell trees before an area is planted rather than when the plants are already growing. Existing trees will get larger and larger, with their roots spreading farther and farther, so take this into consideration before you

plant an area. Often a group of trees shelter one another and, if you thin them out, the remaining ones may blow down. Another option is to leave most of the trees but to limb them up (remove all or most of the lower branches). It is sometimes an eye-opener how much better rhododendrons grow after trees making overhead shade are blown down in storms: initial despair often gives way a few years later to comments like, "the best thing that ever happened to the garden."

In the various rhododendron-growing regions of the world, different trees have been found to to be particularly good for

shading rhododendrons. We have found oak, Scot's pine, larch, *Sorbus*, *Malus*, *Prunus*, and small-leaved maples to be particularly good. *Sorbus* are especially valuable as they bring color into the garden in autumn when rhododendrons are at their least interesting. In North America, many of the native trees such as *Liquidambar*, *Nyssa*, dogwood, hemlock, redwood, pine, hickory, and oak are all excellent subjects. Douglas fir is rather greedy and the constantly shedding

High shade, provided by the native *Sequoia sempervirens*, provide excellent growing conditions for rhododendrons in northern California.

branches tend to damage plants growing beneath them. In Australia, Eucalyptus species, such as *E. regnans*, and *Quercus coccinea* are successful while in New Zealand *Gleditsia* and alder are very good.

In semitropical areas, where Vireyas can be grown outdoors, wonderful combinations of palms, tree ferns, and other local vegetation can be made with the rhododendrons. If the rainfall is high enough, you may be able to plant them on mossy logs. Wherever you garden, the key is always to avoid hungry trees with shallow roots that will compete with those of the rhododendrons. Try to have the minimum canopy possible to give

you the protection you require.

Some collectors (mostly in North America) have decided in favor of artificial shade and shelter for their species collections, constructing lathe houses with wooden or plastic strips. While not as ornamental as natural tree-cover, the fact that the shade is constant, and that there is no competition from tree roots, make this an attractive option to provide light or heavy shade with some heat and frost protection.

As plants of open moorland, alpine rhododendron varieties should ideally be grown in full exposure so that they maintain the compact, mounded shape that they would have in the wild. In shade, such varieties tend to be sparse and drawn and to flower poorly. Unfortunately, alpine varieties, with a few exceptions, are not heat tolerant and particularly dislike having hot roots in summer, so shade is often the only option.

Wind Shelter

Shelter from the prevailing winds is very important for many varieties of rhododendrons. In the U.K., for example, strong, rain-bearing, southwesterly winds and cold, sometimes snow-bearing, easterlies can be severely damaging.

As a general rule, rhododendron varieties with the largest leaves need the most shelter as they can easily have their leaves broken at the petiole and even become completely defoliated. Many species have delicate new growth that is vulnerable to wind damage.

Buildings and walls do, of course, provide shelter, but as solid barriers they also funnel and lift the wind, redirecting it to strike as hard in other directions. The best protection is provided by permeable barriers, such as trees, shrubs, or artificial materials, so that the velocity of the wind is reduced. Rhododendrons shelter one another very well, and the tougher ones can always be planted as a barrier to protect less wind-tolerant vari-

The spectacular new growth of rhododendron species in the author's garden at Glendoick. The varied color of the indumentum on the leaves is evident.

eties. The shelter may take some time to establish and become effective, and in the meantime artificial material, such as plastic netting or plastic strips, may be used.

In coastal gardens, shelter is often absolutely crucial to the success of the garden; ferocious winds laden with salt spray can cause severe damage. In coastal gardens in the U.K., such as Inverewe in Scotland, *Cupressus macrocarpa*, *Pinus muricata*, *Pinus radiata*, *Griselinia littoralis*, *Arbutus unedo*, *Escallonia*, *Olearia*, and many other trees and shrubs are used to create these essential, dense windbreaks.

In colder places, hardier trees and shrubs are required. In areas with harsh winters, strong winds when the ground is frozen can cause severe desiccation of foliage, defoliating and killing plants, while in warm areas, hot winds can cause similar damage. Low-growing and alpine rhododendrons usually require little or no wind-protection (as long as it is not laden with salt spray), since many of them grow in full exposure on mountainsides and passes in their natural environment.

Frost and Cold

Rhododendrons vary greatly in cold hardiness. The hardiest (often known as ironclads) can withstand -25°F (-32°C) or colder, while in contrast, most of the tropical Vireya varieties can withstand little or no frost. Snow, which covers many of the rhododendron species in winter in their native habitats, is an excellent protection from extremes of cold (though its weight can cause breakage), but unfortunately snow does not necessarily coincide with the coldest weather. While it is common policy to select only varieties of certain hardiness for the area you live in, few gardeners can resist attempting to grow one or two that are of borderline hardiness. In this case, selection of site and clever use of shelter is very important.

Even within a small garden, there are microclimates. Walls facing the sun are among the warmest sites, while hollows and the bottom of slopes, where frost settles, are usually among the coldest places. Overhead shade provides a few degrees of protection from late frosts for flowers and emerging young growth.

Many people use forms of artificial protection for their more tender varieties. Beware of leaving such materials on when thawing occurs as it can cause rotting of foliage; all materials used must allow air to circulate. The purpose is as much to moderate temperature fluctuations as it is to protect the plants from extreme cold.

In the Pacific Northwest and even south into California, the most damaging weather is the occasional very sudden drop in temperature in autumn before plants have had time to harden off. Young plants of borderline hardiness are especially vulnerable to cold. A mature plant of the same variety may be able to resprout from the trunk, even after severe damage, whereas a young plant might be killed in those conditions.

At Glendoick, we use several materials to protect young plants from spring and early autumn frosts. Spun polypropylene (available in different widths and thicknesses) is lightweight but gives protection from a few degrees of frost. It is hard to anchor, gets heavy when wet, and must be taken off if snow is forecast.

Better are sheets of opaque corrugated plastic —these are about ⅛–¼ in. (3–5mm) thick and act like double-glazing— which can be bent over to make miniature hoop houses or coldframes. These can be secured so that they will withstand rain, snow, and wind. The only problem is that plants dry out underneath them. Of course, this is simply an extension of the traditional cloche, which is expensive if made of glass, but which is also available in plastic.

Some people place wicker baskets over individual plants overnight. These should come off in daylight hours, unless it is still freezing. Others wrap stems or the whole plant in burlap or sacking, or use conifer branches (including the Christmas tree!). As is explained in the sections on shade (page 16) and shelter (page 19), plants in the open are much more vulnerable than those in a sheltered site, so placing or moving borderline plants to the

The leaves on this *R. wiltonii* show the telltale browning and distortion caused by late frost, which has occurred after the growth buds have started to elongate.

most favorable sites may reduce or eliminate the need for artificial protection.

Spring frosts (and to some extent early autumn frosts) are the bane of rhododendron gardeners in many parts of the world. Few rhododendrons have frost-resistant flowers or new growth, and few rhododendron growers have not experienced the forlorn sight of a specimen in full flower one day, reduced the following morning to a mountain of limp, soggy, gray-brown mush after an overnight frost. Ideas mentioned above can all help prevent such disasters but with severe frost, there is very little that can be done.

Commercial growers in some parts of the world use their sprinkler systems to keep the air moving and prevent frost damage. This can cause flooding and even a garden full of icicle-covered plants, but it does work. Start the watering before the pipes freeze up.

New growth damaged by frost can be cut off. This will usually be replaced by a flush from lateral buds farther down the branches. Potentially most damaging of all is bark split. This is caused by the sap running

in the stem freezing and splitting a branch open. Often, it is not revealed immediately but the damaged plant, or part of the plant, can collapse later in the growing season. Young plants, even hardy varieties, can easily be killed in this way (see page 70).

To summarize: rhododendrons require varying degrees of shade and shelter. The amount depends both on the variety and the climatic conditions to be faced.

Dappled shade provided by birch, conifers, and Japanese maples provides a perfect environment for azaleas at Exbury Gardens, Hampshire, England.

Shade and shelter:
• provides protection from damaging winds.
• moderates the effects of sun on flowers and foliage.
• moderates/reduces soil temperature in summer.
• reduces the damaging effects of spring frosts on growth and flowers.
• reduces the combined stress of frozen ground and sun in winter.
• maintains humidity of atmosphere around plants.

Too much shade:
• encourages drawn and leggy plants.
• inhibits flowering.
• reduces moisture available to rhododendrons (due to tree roots).
• encourages disease such as powdery mildew.

Landscaping with Rhododendrons

Using Rhododendrons in the Landscape

Given the right soil conditions, acidity, drainage, and moisture, rhododendrons are quite accommodating, easily grown, low-maintenance plants. They require no routine pruning, and little or no feeding. As most are evergreens, they can provide a year-round structure to the garden and their foliage can make a fine foil for other plants. Of course, in full flower few plants can equal rhododendrons for quantity of bloom (sometimes virtually hiding the leaves); variety of colors from white to pink, red, purple, yellow, and orange; and range of flower and truss shape, from rounded to hanging and tubular.

With careful selection of varieties you can have rhododendrons that flower around Christmas in milder climates, while at the end of the season, you can still have them in flower in August. Quite a number of rhododendrons have scent. These fall into two categories, those that can generally be cultivated outdoors except in the severest climates and those that, for most of us, need to be grown indoors. In both cases, the flowers are light in color, mostly white or pink, or yellow in the case of *R. luteum.* The hardier (outdoor) ones include the species and hybrids of subsection Fortunea such as *R. decorum, R. fortunei,* and the famous *R. "Loderi"* hybrids; also many species azaleas such as *R. occidentale* and its hybrids like "Irene Koster."

There are several styles of gardening associated with rhododendrons, but they are seldom used in formal plantings. I have, once or twice, seen them trained as standards or clipped into hedges, but generally they do not suit straight lines, order, and regiment. Woodland and rock gardens are imitations of nature and, therefore, are essentially informal. The informality is also a boon in the amount of labor required for upkeep. Much of the weeding, pruning, clipping, edging, and mowing that goes on in other sorts of gardens should be less necessary, especially in the woodland garden.

I leave the vexed question of color coordination to others. The garden design guru Gertrude Jekyll tolerated only small-flowered white rhododendrons, while at the other end of the spectrum, many of the latest hybrids have massive multicolored flowers, which some consider to be vulgar. There are varieties and planting combinations to suit every taste. The great thing about rhododendrons is that you can move them if you find a color combination offensive. The depth of feeling inspired by this subject is extraordinary. The otherwise calm and reasonable rhododendron author David Leach, in his classic *Rhododendrons of the World,* takes exception to one of my favorite rhododendron species thus:

"I advise all readers to turn their eyes from *R. niveum* in its usual dull purple form, which is one of the most degraded, poisonously bilious colors to be found on earth. An ax, not a woodland, is the remedy for its appalling hue."

A spectacular rhododendron walk winds down to the river at Cotehele House and Garden, Cornwall, England.

Foliage Effect

While most of the larger hybrids have fairly standard green leaves, many of the species and some of the smaller hybrids have foliage that gives year-round interest. The leaf's under surface, and sometimes the upper surface too, may be covered in a layer of hairs known as indumentum, varying in color from silver to white, fawn, rufous, or dark brown. The indumentum is often particularly fine on the new growth as it unfurls. Species with this feature include *R. bureauvii*, with a thick reddish-brown layer on the leaf underside, and *R. pachysanthum*, whose indumentum matures from white to fawn to deep reddish-brown.

Sometimes the foliage effect comes from the size of the leaf: those of *R. sinogrande* can be up to 3 ft. (1m) in length. In other cases it is the leaf shape: almost round in *R. williamsianum* and *R. orbiculare*, long and narrow in *R. roxieanum*; or the leaf color, gray-blue in some forms of *R. cinnabarinum* and *R. lepidostylum* and red in culti-

Right: The rare dwarf species *R. pronum* is prized by collectors for its blue leaves and compact habit, despite the fact that it hardly ever flowers.

Below: The emerging new growth of the rare, red-flowered species *R. exasperatum* is a wonderful metallic purple color. This species can be identified by its oval leaves and bristly stems.

vars such as "Elizabeth Lockhart." The new growth of rhododendrons is very variable and often very showy, almost as good as a second flowering. Species with colored new growth include forms of *R. keiskei*, *R. lutescens* (both red), *R. decorum*, and *R. williamsianum* (bronzy). Other species have showy red leaf-buds scales (which protect the resting buds through the winter) and are displayed as the new

leaves unfurl. Good examples are *R. fortunei* and *R. falconeri*. Many species have outstanding peeling or smooth, colored bark. Some of the finest include *R. thomsonii* and *R. hodgsonii*.

How Far Apart Should I Plant?

Occasionally, one finds a wonderful old specimen plant growing out on its own, with no competition from other plants or trees. This has formed a perfect shape and is the envy of everyone who sees it. Such plants are the exception, not the rule. Individual specimens, planted on lawns, for instance, tend to be buffeted by wind, to dry out, and to have weeds or grass growing at their roots.

Rhododendrons are sociable plants and unless you are prepared to put in the extra work required, do not dot them around too much. Conversely, planting too densely is also to be avoided: there are many once fine collections now reduced to a few spindly branches competing for light, with the handful of flowers high up and far out of reach. Planting close together for quick impact is fine if you are prepared to move them or thin them later but, in my experience, this is easier

said than done. A garden I visited recently was so over-planted that the paths had completely disappeared under the rhododendrons. In optimum conditions, rhododendrons live for a very long time: 100 years is quite common. Plant with one eye on posterity and you will not regret it.

The size dimensions given in the Plant Directory (see page 80) are very approximate and apply to plants aged 10–20 years. The rainfall, amount of fertilizer used, and length of growing season are all important factors. Often rhododendrons grow as wide as they are high, and there is a limit to the pruning you can do with many of them (see page 51). If you can spare the space, let the really large species grow into fully clothed, rounded specimens. With the small-leaved and dwarf varieties, letting them grow into one another fairly quickly is the best plan.

Primulas are often associated with rhododendrons in the wild as well as in cultivation. Here candelabra primulas are planted in front of R. cerasinum.

Companion Planting

For the majority of gardeners who have limited space to work with, and a desire for year-round interest, rhododendrons will be used with all sorts of other plants for company. The golden rule here is to try to avoid too much competition for moisture. This can come either from below, in the case of greedy tree roots, or from above, in the case of ground cover. As rhododendrons are moisture-loving but shallow-rooted, they will tend to lose the battle and their health will suffer.

In choosing smaller trees, consider both the ultimate size and spread and the season of interest. As rhododendrons are predominantly plants of spring display, plants for autumn and winter are invaluable. In moderate climates such as the U.K. and the Pacific Northwest of North America, there is a huge range of choices for trees and shrubs. *Sorbus* species are particularly good, as they are not hungry feeders, provide filtered shade, and have long-lasting berries of white, yellow, pink, orange, or red. *Eucryphia* is another fine choice; these have very showy white flowers in late summer and early autumn. The hardiest forms are *E.* x *intermedia* "Rostrevor," *E. glutinosa,* and *E.* x *nymanensis.*

They should be planted in full sun and tend to flower on the sunny side of the tree only. Japanese maples (*Acer japonicum* and *Acer palmatum* cultivars) act as a wonderful foil for the foliage of rhododendrons, and many have the bonus of autumn color.

Winter color can be provided by *Mahonia*, winter jasmine, *Viburnum*, and *Hamamelis mollis*, as well as perennials and bulbs such as hellebores and snowdrops.

In severe climates, use a mixture of native and hardy exotics. There are many Japanese and North American natives such as *Styrax, Hamamelis, Cercis, Amelanchier, Halesia,* and *Stewartia* that provide filtered shade, fine flowers, and/or autumn color and whose roots are not too greedy. Some of these thrive only in areas with hot summers. *Kalmia, Leucothoe, Vaccinium,* and other Ericaceous plants enjoy similar soil conditions to rhododendrons and provide interest after the main period of rhododendron flowering.

Above:
R. kiusianum is a fine plant for the rock garden, accompanying small perennials and other plants.

Right: An undulating carpet of many species and hybrid dwarf rhododendrons in the author's garden at Glendoick, Scotland.

The Woodland Garden

28

This style of gardening, developed as a naturalistic way of informal planting through woodland, often up a valley with a stream running through it or around a pond or lake, has become the most popular way to display rhododendrons on a larger scale.

Many of the great rhododendron collections of the south and west of England, such as Exbury and Leonardslee, and in Argyll, Scotland, such as Crarae, are examples of woodland gardens. The development of this gardening style coincided with, and indeed was largely inspired by, the flood of new rhododendron species from the Himalayas and China from 1850 onward; it soon became apparent that many other plants from the Sino-Himalayan region also suited this method of cultivation.

The large foliage of *R. sinogrande* (in the foreground) contrasts well with the pink hybrid "Atroflo" and the white *Prunus avium* in the background.

The essential character of the woodland garden is the informal nature of the winding paths through both native and exotic trees, underplanted with rhododendrons and other shrubs, often with a layer of wild flowers, bulbs, and other smaller plants carpeting the ground underneath. Using contours and bridges to provide paths at different levels allows rhododendrons to be viewed from above and below. The steep slopes at Bodnant, North Wales, and the bridges over the burn at Crarae, Scotland are good examples.

Woodland conditions, with shelter and filtered shade, are essential for varieties of borderline hardiness; at Glendoick, the most favorable sites allow us to grow *R. lindleyi* and *R. sinogrande*, which would not be hardy in the open. Woodland, especially if on a slope with frost drainage, will allow protection from several degrees of frost and often will make the difference between damage to flowers and foliage, and escaping from it.

Although predominantly a British development, this style of

woodland gardening has also been used in other areas with great effect, such as the University of British Columbia Botanic Garden's Asian garden. Exploit your native plants as part of the magic. Pukeiti in North Island, New Zealand, is a good example of native woodland filled with indigenous trees and tree ferns, interplanted with rhododendron species. Particularly fine there are tender species, such as *R. elliottii* and *R. protistum*, which thrive in the luxuriant shelter growing in the high rainfall.

Obviously, few people are lucky enough to be able to garden on the grand scale that woodland gardening implies: many of these gardens cover acres and can take hours to walk around. However, the basic tenets of woodland gardening—informality, shade, shelter, and plant associations—apply equally well in smaller gardens. The most satisfactory displays of healthy rhododendrons in small and medium-sized gardens are often those that have adapted the principles of the woodland garden landscape.

In the U.K., the dominant feature of most

woodland gardens is their rhododendrons, but certain other genera are conspicuous too. The best larger shade trees to associate with rhododendrons are discussed under shade and shelter on pages 16 and 19. The ideal is a mixture of conifers and hardwoods. In our west of Scotland garden, Baravalla, the natural woodland is oak, hazel, and birch with a few mature fir trees that seed themselves.

At Glendoick, we have lost our dominant tree, the elm, from Dutch elm disease, leaving a mixture of larch, Douglas fir, sycamore, and beech with an undergrowth of elder (*Sambucus nigra*) and other plants. In choosing trees, consider the bark as well as the flowers, foliage, and berries. *Betula utilis* and *B. jacquemontii* have fine reddish-brown and white, peeling bark respectively. Other species with interesting bark include *Prunus serrula*, *Acer griseum*, *A. hersii*, and other snakebark maples.

Magnolias are another obvious choice. On the large scale in relatively mild climates, the massive-growing *Magnolia campbellii* and its relatives give a spectacular display in early spring. On a smaller scale, use other species such as the summer-flowering *M. wilsonii* and hybrids such as "Leonard Messel."

In eastern North America, many of the new hybrid magnolias put on a spectacular display in the few weeks before the main

Attractive though the combination is between Dicentra and Rhododendron, the ground cover can very easily get out of control in a small garden.

rhododendron blooming period. Magnolias are rather greedy feeders, so avoid planting rhododendrons directly underneath them in areas of low rainfall. Camellias are another mainstay companion plant, especially in the gardens of Cornwall. If you can obtain *Embothrium coccineum*, the fiery orange flowers of this South American native provide a fine contrast to the colors of the rhododendrons.

Pieris thrive in considerable shade and there are now many different forms with red, pink, or white flowers, red or bronze young growth, and some have variegated leaves.

These, and *Enkianthus*, are both members of the Ericaceae, the same family as rhododendrons, so they enjoy similar growing conditions. As well as their attractive hanging flowers, *Enkianthus* have among the most spectacular autumn color with red, orange, and yellow tones. Other plants with good autumn foliage are *Rhododendron luteum* (otherwise known as *Azalea pontica*), *Euonymous alatus*, Japanese maples, and *Sassafras*.

Meconopsis, particularly the blue poppies *M. betonicifolia*, *M. grandis*, and their hybrid *M. x sheldonii*, prefer moist, cool woodland: they are a struggle to grow in areas with summer heat and low rainfall. Some of the monocarpic varieties such as the *M. napalensis* or *M. regia* hybrids are more suited to hotter and drier conditions. Other fine companion plants include *Trillium*, *Erythronium*, *Helleborus*, *Cardiocrinum*, and *Lilium*.

Most woodland gardeners encourage wild flowers by avoiding mowing or scything until mid-summer, when most of the flowers are over. At Glendoick we have many native British plants that thrive among the rhododendrons; these include *Meconopsis cambrica* (the Welsh poppy), species of *Brunnera* and *Digitalis* (foxgloves), as well as several varieties of ferns.

Berries can be provided by trees and shrubs such as *Vaccinium*, *Gaultheria* (which now includes *Pernettya mucronata*), *Cotoneaster*, and *Sorbus*. North American natives such as *Styrax* and *Halesia* have showy flowers and provide dappled shade. Bamboos are often found in association with rhododendrons in the wild and can be used effectively in cultivation. The best are the taller-growing, clump-forming types such as *Fargesia murieliae* (syn. *Arundinaria murieliae*).

Beware of the very rampant, spreading species such as the tall *Sasa palmata* and the low growing *Sasaella ramosa* (syn. *Arundinaria vagans*). These need lots of space, though they can be kept in bounds with artificial barriers in the soil. Most woodland gardens contain sites too dry for rhododendrons. These can be filled with shrubs such as *Ilex*, *Deutzia*, *Philadelphus*, *Viburnum*, *Ribes*, and *Hypericum*. All of these associate with rhododendrons in the wild, as do climbers such as *Schisandra* and *Clematis montana*.

The best woodland gardens have extensive underplantings of bulbs

The flowering cherry and other trees provide ideal dappled shade for the underplantings of azaleas and rhododendrons at Leonardslee Gardens in Surrey, England.

and herbaceous plants. Here the key is to use plants that are subtle rather than garish, to keep the "natural" look of the garden. In the wild, rhododendrons are often associated with *Primula* and *Meconopsis*, which make ideal companion plants in areas with fairly cool summers. The easiest primulas to establish and naturalize are the candelabra types such as *Primula japonica*, *P. helodoxa*, *P. bulleana*, and *P. poissoni*. These tend to hybridize and produce seedlings of a huge range of colors.

The Rhododendron Border

Some may well argue that a border planted only with rhododendrons and azaleas is monotonous, particularly when they are out of flower. I would certainly agree that it can be, especially if you exclusively plant the larger hybrids, which look very similar to one another without blooms. With dwarf and medium-sized growers, if you garden in a moderate climate (winter minimum 0°F [-18°C]), you can plant rhododendron borders that do remain interesting all year round. In such a border, I would tend to use plants with an ultimate height of up to 6 ft. (2m) at the back, gradually sloping down to low-growing varieties at the front. The great advantage of not mixing in other plants is that the conditions can be made to suit the rhododendrons ideally in terms of soil, drainage, feeding, and watering.

In nature, rhododendrons and azaleas are usually found in clumps and colonies, sheltering and shading each other's roots. In the garden, imitate this by allow-

Japanese maples and Japanese azaleas produce a marvelous show in the Valley Gardens at Windsor Great Park, England.

ing the rhododendrons to grow into one another, forming an undulating carpet. Before the individual plants start to join up, you can use preemergence herbicides to keep down the weeds. On a larger scale or for quick impact, plant three or more of each variety so that they can form large clumps. We often do this with dwarf varieties grown from wild seed, so that we can display the variation within a species.

Most people want as long and spectacular a flowering season as possible. With careful choice, the year can begin in winter with *R. lapponicum* and *R. dauricum* and end with late-flowering evergreen azaleas such as *R. naka-harae* in early and mid-summer, with a more or less continuous display in between.

Flower shape, size, and color should also be considered. The rounded trusses of the "yak" hybrids are very different from the bells of the *R. williamsianum* hybrids, for instance. In frost pockets, choose early-flowering varieties such as "Ptarmigan" and "Christmas Cheer," which open their flowers over a long period. This ensures that if flowers are spoiled by frost, more will open later. Most "yak" hybrids as well as evergreen and deciduous azaleas are late

enough flowering to avoid spring frost danger. In milder gardens, you can have scent from some of the Maddenia species and hybrids. In colder climates some of the species and hybrids (mostly large-growing) and many of the deciduous azaleas, such as *R. luteum*, can provide the perfume.

Always consider the importance of foliage when planning a rhododendron border. After all, the flowers last only a few weeks while fine foliage is always on display. Choose a variety of leaf shapes, from the rounded and oval *R. williamsianum* and its hybrids such as "Gartendirektor Rieger," "Linda," and "Osmar," to those with narrow or long leaves such as *R. roxieanum* and *R. elegantulum*. Leaf size is also important. The larger-leaved hybrids such as "Unique" and some of the "yaks" contrast well with those at the other end of the scale, such as the tiny *R. calostrotum ssp. keleticum* Radicans group, which has some of the smallest and narrowest leaves of all. The texture of the leaf itself can provide interest. The hybrid "Rubicon" has deeply ribbed, dark green leaves, while these of *R. thomsonii* are completely smooth and flat. Many dwarf and medium-sized species and a few hybrids have a magnificent indumentum. This is usually on the leaf underside, but in some species, such as

R. pachysanthum, R. pseudochrysanthum, R. yakushimanum, and several others, the silvery dusting on the new growth persists all summer, giving a most attractive effect. In many other varieties the white, silver, fawn, or brown indumentum on the upper leaf surface is only temporary; good examples are the "yak" hybrids such as "Hydon Dawn," "Sleepy," and "Ken Janeck."

Exploit the colored foliage of *R. lepidostylum, R. fastigiatum,* and *R. campanulatum ssp. aeruginosum* (glaucous-blue) or "Elizabeth Lockhart" and "Elizabeth Red Foliage" (reddish-purple) or "Ponticum Variegatum" and "Goldflimmer" (variegated).

Many species have very showy new growth, giving almost a "second flowering." Some of the best include the bronzy and purplish new leaves of *R. williamsianum* and its hybrids and the red young growth of forms of *R. keiskei* and *R. lutescens.*

Good autumn color can be provided by deciduous azaleas such as *R. luteum,* which can be placed at the back of a border, or *R. dauricum, R. mucronulatum,* and their hybrids. Many varieties have leaves that turn to rich, deep reds, purples, and mahogany in winter. Some of the best include the "P.J.M." Group in its various forms as well as many of the evergreen or Japanese azaleas.

The Mixed Border

In smaller gardens, where space is at a premium, the aim is usually for maximum impact and year-round interest provided by mixed borders. Usually a structure of shrubs, both deciduous and evergreen, is interspaced and underplanted with perennials and even annuals.

As usual, the key is to avoid greedy and invasive plants. Roses and heathers are two examples that will dry out and impoverish the soil at the expense of the rhododendrons. Often a part of the garden, or a particular bed, will be selected for acid-loving plants: other Ericaceous plants, such as *Pieris, Kalmia latifolia, Leucothoe,* as well as shrubs such as camellias, hydrangea, and Japanese maples.

A lot of the choices for mixed plantings are questions of taste. I have seen some bizarre and outrageous combinations with bulbs such as tulips, bedding plants, and rhododendrons growing together. Purists will be appalled and others will love the effect. As most

A riot of color in a New Zealand garden with deciduous azaleas and rhododendrons along with annuals and perennials.

rhododendrons are evergreen, they provide much of the permanent structure of the mixed border, especially in winter when the perennials have died down and the deciduous shrubs have only bare stems. Because of this it is well worth considering the foliage and growth habit of the varieties you choose

as much as the flower. Planting the rhododendrons in clumps so that they can grow into one another and shade one another's roots will cut down on the need for weeding and watering. How close you can plant to trees and hedges depends on your rainfall and whether you can provide artificial watering. Some of the subsection Triflora species will withstand relatively dry conditions once established.

Rock Gardens

The best way to display dwarf and alpine rhododendrons is in a rock garden. Here, the alpine varieties are grown in an imitation of their wild state on moorland or rocky slopes. Such plantings should be out in the open, away from trees, allowing the dwarf plants to maintain their natural compact shape. Let the plants grow into one another, forming an undulating mat of foliage textures, leaving occasional patches of bare ground in which to plant bulbs and alpine perennials.

The best rock gardens have natural or artificial contours, imitating the mountain slopes where the plants grow wild. As well as dwarf rhododendrons, rock gardens are ideal for other low-growing Ericaceae such as *Phyllodoce* with pink or creamy-white bells, *Cassiope* with tiny white bells, *Kalmiopsis* and its hybrid *x Phylliopsis* with pink flowers, and dwarf *Gaultheria, Andromeda, Gaylussacia,* and *Vaccinium.* Dwarf bulbs and alpines such as *Rhodohypoxis, Primula, Corydalis, Nomocharis, Fritillaria,* and smaller ground orchids are all excellent choices.

This peat moss border contains a fine choice of plants to associate with dwarf rhododendrons and azaleas. The bright red azalea is "Vuyk's Scarlet" surrounded by *Pieris*, *Phyllodoce*, *Lilium*, and *Trillium*.

At Glendoick we have found by bitter experience that certain bulbs and perennials are too invasive and soon get out of control. For us, these included *Muscari, Chionodoxa, Crocus,* and bluebells, all of which can be almost impossible to eradicate. In different climates, other plants will probably be equally troublesome. In rock gardens, rhododendrons and dwarf azaleas can form a dominant part, or just be scattered through a mixed planting of assorted alpines.

Natural rock gardens on windswept Himalayan mountains give plenty of ideas on how to garden with such plants as are found there. Those that require excellent drainage grow on scree, others that require more moisture grow in snowmelt. Some species prefer full exposure while others grow in the lee of rocks, which provide wind shelter and help to retain moisture. Imitate these habitats in gardens, using scree beds, planting species next to rocks to protect new growth from prevailing winds, and making use of moisture-retaining crevices to keep roots damp and cool.

Growing in Containers

Rhododendrons in containers, whether outside or indoors, need a fairly free-draining and open, but at the same time moisture-retentive, compost. This is not a contradiction and is essential for healthy plants. Rhododendrons cannot survive for long with dry roots but, equally, if the compost is too soggy and the water in the pot becomes stagnant, then chlorotic foliage and poor growth, or even death through root-rot (*Phytophthora*) may result. A mixture of fairly coarse bark and peat moss, sometimes with added perlite, needles, or woodchips, is the ideal combination for container rhododendrons indoors or out.

The heavily scented hybrid "Fragrantissimum" is commonly grown in a container, which can be taken into the house when in flower. Here, the clay pot is raised off the ground to ensure free drainage.

The first two substances, either singly or together, are used by most commercial growers of rhododendrons in containers. The easiest option for feeding in containers is the slow-release granules, lasting up to 18 months. These can be either incorporated into the compost or clusters can be pushed into the soil of plants already in containers. Otherwise, granular or liquid feeding can be applied from late spring to midsummer. Do not go on feeding longer or growth will continue at the expense of flower buds.

Rhododendrons should not be over-potted. If anything, they grow and flower better if slightly pot-bound, as long as they are well fed and watered. Be ware of shallow, pan shaped pots due to the physical properties of water in containers: all pots tend to have a soggy layer at the bottom and this layer should not come into contact with the roots. All containers need adequate drainage holes and you may have to make extra ones, especially for Vireyas and Maddenia. I have seen excellent results, indoors and out, of rhododendrons growing in slices of tree-fern logs, which may be available in places such as Australia, New Zealand, and similar mild climates. Many rhododendrons are epiphytic in the wild and this method imitates that habitat. Beware of the fungal disease *Phytophthora* in containers, which is caused by a combination of poor drainage and high soil temperatures and is lethal (see page 68).

Outdoors

Many of the saddest-looking rhododendrons I have ever seen were in containers outside town houses. These straggly, yellow and brown-leaved sentinels were expending the last months of their short lives pushing out the odd feeble flower, before expiring, unloved and abandoned.

It is certainly possible to grow fine rhododendrons in containers but only if you are prepared to maintain them properly. They require more attention than those in the ground; they need repotting every few years together with regular feeding and watering. There are several reasons why containers may be the best or only option for growing rhododendrons. Many people have no garden but have perhaps some hard space suitable for pots. Others have gardens with alkaline or heavy clay soil. The fine foliage and compact habit of "yak" hybrids are among the best choices, as they look good for 12 months of the year and their new growth, often silvery, adds interest when flowering is past.

By all means put other plants in your containers with the rhododendrons, but avoid those such as ground covers with greedy root systems, which will compete for moisture and nutrients. Bulbs, noninvasive alpines, and bedding plants can all be used successfully.

Rhododendrons (especially evergreen azaleas) are one of the most popular subjects for bonsai. There are thousands of varieties of Satsuki and other azaleas bred in Japan for this purpose, but they need winter protection in colder and more northern climates.

As with many other plants, the foliage of rhododendrons will tolerate much colder temperatures than the roots, which are usually killed at 10–20°F (5–10°C). In the ground, the snow can actually create a layer of insulation, preventing the soil from getting as cold as the air above. Plants in containers do not have this insulation and the roots, usually pressed against the inside of the pot, are very vulnerable to being hard frozen, which can kill an otherwise hardy plant. If you cannot bring your containers indoors in the severest weather, then it is worth taking other precautions. Insulation with polystyrene, bubble-plastic, straw, or similar materials will help. Placing your containers so they are all touching and then insulating the outside of the block, is a practice followed by nurseries. Alternatively, dig the container into the ground so that the surrounding soil insulates it, which also stops the container from blowing over.

The many varieties of Japanese or evergreen azaleas make ideal subjects for bonsai.

Indoors

Unless you live in the milder areas where rhododendrons are cultivated, for example, western Britain, France, California, Australia, or New Zealand, the more tender rhododendrons need to be grown indoors, at least during the winter. Indica, or tender azaleas, are the only part of the genus rhododendron that make good "house" plants, as they can put up with the low light levels coupled with warm winter temperatures and dry air of the home. Maddenia and Vireyas really need a greenhouse or conservatory with plenty of light, cool winter temperatures, and a fairly high humidity. Maddenia species and hybrid plants can be brought into the house in flower and can stay in for a week or two, as long as they are kept fairly cool, but Vireyas can stand only a day or two.

The new greenhouse at Windsor Great Park, England, where the whole front can be opened in summer, gives the best of both worlds as it allows cool summer temperatures and frost protection in winter.

Soils and Planting

Soils: Acid or Alkaline?

Rhododendrons have several basic requirements:
1 Acid soil.
2 A loose/coarse organic planting medium which allows air circulation around the roots. Compacted and heavy clay soils are very poor for rhododendron culture.
3 Sufficient moisture at the roots during the growing season.
4 Many early-flowering, larger leaved tender varieties benefit from a certain amount of shelter, especially from wind. In more southerly locations, where summer sun is strong, for instance in North America, many rhododendrons require considerable shade for best results.

Acidity in soil is measured in terms of its pH—pH 7 is neutral. Lower numbers are acid and higher numbers are alkaline. Most rhododendrons enjoy a pH of between 4 and 6, and ideally between 4.5 and 5.5. On chalky, limy, or alkaline soils, where water is very hard, rhododendrons grow poorly or not at all. The reasons for this are complex, but essentially soil pH affects the availability of nutrients and the health of essential micro-organisms, thereby hindering photosynthesis.

Some rhododendrons do actually grow on limestone in the wild but this is usually in areas of high rainfall and the limestone is dolomitic (contains magnesium). This apparently accounts for the fact that the plants are not poisoned by taking up too much calcium, though the exact mechanisms are still not completely understood. There are various ways of determining the pH of soil. It can be analyzed professionally, or with a soil test kit or pH meter purchased from a garden center. Ensure that soil samples are taken from several sites in the garden as pH can vary considerably even within a small area. The important thing to ascertain if you have alkaline soil is whether it is artificially (and therefore temporarily) so, or whether the area you live in is genuinely alkaline. In areas with naturally acid soil, the pH may have been raised by artificial means. Both farmers and vegetable gardeners often lime their soil routinely to increase yield. In this case, the lime will be washed out over several years, so the high pH is not a great worry. Sometimes the materials of house building and hard landscaping such as rubble, cement, and mortar will result in pockets of soil having a high pH.

The bold colors of evergreen azaleas brighten up a large-scale rock garden, filled with an enormous variety of plant material.

Raised Beds

Raised beds are used to isolate the growing medium of the rhododendrons and other acid lovers from the natural garden soil. Beds are usually lined with heavy polyethylene or similar material, and filled with acidic topsoil from elsewhere, or a compost made up from peat moss, bark, and other acidic organic matter. It is most important to ensure good drainage. A flat, polyethylene-lined bed can all too easily become a muddy swimming pool in wet weather, conditions which rhododendrons will not tolerate! Where possible, the lining should be sloped so that excess water can drain out from the front, back, or sides. Where this is not possible, fill the bottom layer of the bed with coarse, free-draining material such as crushed rock or gravel, or even build small drains or runoffs.

The bed should be 12 in. (30cm) or more in depth so that the roots are not in contact with the lining. The sides of the bed can be of any suitable materials: wood, bricks, peat moss blocks, or parts of walls. The bed must be watered with rainwater or artificially acidified water. Many people collect rainwater for this purpose. To cut down on evaporation, it is well worth applying a mulch to the surface of a raised bed (see page 43).

There are several varieties of rhododendron that can tolerate more or less neutral soil. *R. hirsutum* grows only on limestone in its native European Alps and dislikes very acid soil. Varieties for near neutral soil:
Species. *R. augustinii*, *R. rubiginosum*, *R. decorum*, *R. hirsutum*, *R. sanguineum* ssp. *didymum*, *R. vernicosum*.
Hybrids: "Cunningham's White," "Puncta."

An important breakthrough for alkaline or neutral soil-tolerant rhododendrons has been developed recently in Germany and has been launched on the market. German growers have long known that benefits such as easier culture can be obtained by grafting rhododendrons onto selected rootstocks. A rootstock called INKARHO®, which grows well in pH 5.5–7, has been bred and popular hybrids are now being grafted onto it and should gradually become available. As yet it has been tested only in northern Europe, where apparently it is very promising.

Chlorotic leaves are a good indicator. Usually the easiest and quickest way to ascertain the natural soil pH of an area is to look for telltale plants. Rhododendrons (including azaleas) and other members of the family Ericaceae, such as heathers, are a good indicator, as are blue Hortensia hydrangeas. Conversely, a lack of acid-loving plants in the area and hard water (which does not lather) in the taps are two very obvious clues to alkalinity. A few words over the fence to anyone with a good garden will soon give you all the information you need.

What to do if you have neutral or alkaline soil?
Neutral soil or artificially limed soil can be acidified by mixing in a percentage of peat moss. Alternatively, sulphur powder or iron sulphate can be applied. To reduce an area of soil of 216 ft.^{2} (20m^2) by one pH unit (from pH7 to pH6, for instance) requires approximately 3½ lb. (1.5kg) of iron sulphate.

These substances are fertilizers with high concentrations of nitrogen and need to be used very sparingly among growing plants. Alternatively, use strong doses but hold off planting for several months so that the nitrogen has time to leach out of the soil. Iron chelates (sequestrols) can be used to treat plants with an iron deficiency chlorosis caused by too high a pH.

This is quite an expensive and temporary way to solve the problem. All too often, even gardening experts prescribe sequestrols to cure any yellow-leaved rhododendron. In 19 times out of 20, I am convinced that the yellow leaves will be caused by lack of fertilizer, poor drainage, over-deep planting, or drought rather than a soil pH/iron problem. Of course, if the water in your area is hard, the acidified soil will gradually return to an alkaline state. In this case, growing in raised beds or containers (see page 34) is probably a better option.

In areas with alkaline soil (and water), it is possible to grow rhododendrons in a raised bed. Such beds must be watered with rainwater rather than tapwater to maintain acidity.

Types of Soil

Soil types are usually defined by the particle size that they contain. Soils with the largest particle size are sands. These have excellent drainage but poor retention of water and nutrients. At the other end of the scale are clays, which have microscopically small particles and very good water and mineral retentive properties but are often slow draining and compacted, preventing aeration for the roots. Loams are made up of a combination of these particle sizes and are the ideal basis for a growing medium for rhododendrons, being well aerated but moisture retentive and able to hold nutrients. The type of soil can be ascertained both by the appearance and feel, the weight of it, and by digging a hole and filling it with water. Clay soils tend to have very slow drainage while in sandy soils, the water drains too quickly.

Almost all soils are best improved artificially for optimum growing conditions; for rhododendrons heavy clay or very sandy soils will normally require the most work. Clay soils should be improved by the addition of inert materials such as sand or perlite or, better, the use of organic matter such as leaf mold and composted bark. The soil should be worked in fairly dry conditions and compacted clay can be broken up by exposure to frost. Soils with poor drainage encourage the potentially lethal fungal disease *Phytophthora*. Certain varieties are particularly sensitive to this (many species and most yellow hybrids, for instance) and it is prevalent in areas with hot summers (see page 68).

Sandy soils also benefit from the addition of organic matter and in this case peat moss can be added to the list, as it has excellent moisture retention. A thick mulch to cut down evaporation is also useful on light or sandy soils.

Top: Well-rotted leaf mold is one of the finest organic materials, especially that from oak and beech trees.

Center: Conifer needles are an excellent organic material as they help prevent soil compaction, allowing plenty of air to the roots.

Bottom: Composted bark is one of the finest organic materials for soil improvement, propagation, and as an ingredient for container composts.

Organic Matter

There is no doubt that thorough soil preparation pays dividends when trying to establish newly planted rhododendrons. It is astonishing how many people are prepared to invest a lot of money in plants but are reluctant to spend anything on soil improvement with organic matter.

Partially rotted leaf mold from the previous year's leaf fall is an excellent medium and may well be available for nothing. Composted bark can be bought by the bag or by the truck load. We make very good organic matter at Glendoick by chipping conifer trimmings (from *Cupressocyparis leylandii* hedges, for instance) and letting them compost for a year.

General garden compost or, on a larger scale, composted straw, green waste, sawdust, wood chips, newspaper, and other substances have been used successfully. All these contribute to soil aeration and moisture retention as well as providing nutrients as they rot down. There have been some disasters—I do not recommend using large quantities of a new source of organic matter until it has been tested on a small scale, especially if you are not sure of the source or exact ingredients and age of the material. In the case of bark, sawdust, and wood chips, extra nitrogen is required as these substances use large amounts in the breaking down process and the soil soon becomes nitrogen-starved. All are best left to compost for several months or longer, before being used.

Sawdust can be a good medium but it can also be a curse. In the Pacific Northwest of North America, the sawdust from the Douglas Fir seems to be of a consistent standard and is commonly and successfully used in huge quantities by nurseries to raise field-grown rhododendrons. The downside of sawdust is that over the years it can rot down to a fine sludge with very poor drainage. It also seems to be a substance that encourages the dreaded *Phytophthora cinnamoni*. Outside the Pacific Northwest, I would only add a small percentage of sawdust to your soil mix due to the variability both of tree source and degree of composting (and therefore fertilizer requirement).

Top: Peat is an acid, moisture-retentive material which is much used in cultivation.

Above: Needles, composted bark, and leaf mold provide the ideal combination of organic matter to mix with garden soil for rhododendrons.

The one substance definitely to avoid is lawn-clippings; the ferocious heat and chemical by-products of composting grass have killed whole collections!

We find that the ideal growing medium is a combination of garden soil with a generous mixture of several of the above substances mixed into the planting area. Think about preparing an area large enough for the rootball of the future rather than just a small hole large enough for the root at time of purchase. Individually prepared holes are fine for large-growing varieties, but smaller ones may benefit from having a whole bed made up for them.

Planting Procedures

Rhododendrons are shallow-rooted plants and must not be planted too deeply. The top of the rootball should be just below the soil surface. The roots that feed the plant are usually just near the top, and rarely more than 1 ft. (30cm) below the surface. If roots are buried deeper, they tend to die off. In heavier soils, loosen the soil up to a considerable depth below where the rootball will be to ensure that it is not left sitting on a hard pan.

The advice given when planting most shrubs, to put fertilizer at the bottom of the hole (e.g., bonemeal) will not do any harm, but is largely a waste of time because there are few feeding roots on the underside of the rootball. When planting any rhododendron, remove weeds and improve the soil in an area considerably larger than the existing rootball, so that there is ample surrounding soil for the new roots to grow into easily. As they are so shallowly rooted, it is advisable to keep the area over the roots free of weeds and other competition for moisture. For the same reason, it is usually not a good idea to plant rhododendrons singly in holes cut into lawns, where they will be competing with the grass.

When planting on steep slopes, especially in areas of low rainfall and on very well-drained soils, it may be necessary to plant in a saucer-like depression so that rainwater and artificial irrigation is allowed to collect and soak into the ground around the rootball. Conversely, in mild climates, where rainfall is very high or the ground is heavy clay, considerable success can be had by planting the rhododendrons on the soil surface itself and mounding up a compost high in organic matter around the plant for the roots to grow into. It may take a while to establish plants in these conditions.

When to Plant

Rhododendrons have compact, fibrous, and shallow rootballs allowing them to be planted and moved at any time of year. I have heard of gardeners (admittedly with good irrigation systems) moving their plants around in full flower to ensure the best color combinations. Having said this, there is no doubt that autumn planting allows the best establishment of plants, especially for large plantings. The warmth of the soil will allow a little root growth before the onset of the severest weather and the winter rains will wash soil well into contact with the rootball. These conditions allow the plant to develop new roots in early spring, which penetrate the surrounding soil before growth starts above ground. This provides a degree of drought resistance and ensures the best possible growth in the first growing season (usually leading to

PLANTING SEQUENCE

1: After the organic matter has been mixed into the soil (see page 44), a hole larger and deeper than the rootball should be dug out and then backfilled. This ensures good drainage. Make sure that the rootball is moist right through. If it is dry, soak it for a while.

2: Make sure the top of the rootball is more or less level with the soil surface. Do not plant too deep. Soil should be firmed up well around the rootball, but do not press down much on the rootball itself, as this compacts the soil underneath and impedes drainage.

3: Unless the soil is already soaking wet (which would indicate less-than-ideal planting conditions), water the newly planted rhododendron thoroughly.

1

the best flowering too). The exception to this is in very severe climates, such as the northeastern U.S.A. and eastern Canada and parts of northern Europe. Here, it is probably preferable to plant in late spring so that the plant has a full growing season *in situ* before having to brave the winter.

Prepare the planting area in summer or early autumn when weeds respond to weedkillers and the ground is dry enough to work easily without compacting the soil. If you are not yet ready to plant, you can cover the prepared area with polyethylene to keep heavy rain and weed seeds out until later.

Planting stages
Remove weeds, with weedkillers if necessary (see page 50), from the planting area.

Prepare the soil. This normally requires the addition of organic matter, as discussed previously, over an area wider and deeper than the rootball.

Make sure the rootball of the plant is moist right through. Soak it in a bucket of water if necessary. A dry rootball will repel water once it has been planted and the plant will languish or die.

Do not plant the rhododendron too deep. Just cover the rootball and no more. Firm up the soil thoroughly around the roots but do not compress the rootball itself. This just compacts the soil under the plant and impairs the drainage.

Unless the soil is very wet, water thoroughly. This helps settle the soil around the rootball.

It is often useful to mulch the area over the rootball (see over).

Mulching

Mulching involves putting a layer or barrier of suitable material on top of the rootball of a plant or plants. A mulch can be of many different substances: chipped bark, wood chips, compost, grit, old newspaper, or old carpets.

This can have several benefits: it can cut down evaporation (lessening the need for watering), keep the roots cool in hot weather and insulated from frost in cold weather, and to discourage weeds from growing over the rootball. There can be disadvantages too: It can prevent the rain penetrating the soil and it can tend to provide a hiding place for insects such as vine weevil.

Different mulches have different attributes. In our woodland garden we mulch in midwinter with the leaf litter left around after leaf fall, coupled with general prunings, compost, twigs from storm damage, and so on. Beech and oak leaf molds are particularly good, while sycamore, lime, and horse chestnut are less suitable as the resulting leaf mold is slimy at first and powdery later, and can even be alkaline. Leaves from these trees should be mixed with oak and beech.

There are many many materials that work. Old carpets are a favorite of the organic gardening

2

fraternity but they are hardly something that is readily at hand, they look dreadful, and they do not allow water to penetrate. Bark and wood chips are excellent for keeping down weeds but they take nitrogen out of the soil as they break down, so you may need to apply extra fertilizer. I recommend not using these substances fresh as they heat up as they compost and may also release undesirable chemicals.

We have recently started using sheets of old newspaper for mulching around small and fussy plants. Several layers can be laid on the surface of the soil. Water it until it becomes soggy and plant through the paper. Then cover with a thin layer of bark or wood chips to improve the appearance. This is especially good for keeping down weeds for the first year when plants are very small, and it cuts down on watering.

I should put in a word here about using peat moss as a mulch. Many garden center labels give the advice "mulch with peat moss once a year when you buy a rhododendron." This is pretty useless advice and I cannot think of any good reason to do it. Peat moss has no nutrients, repels

3

water, and tends to dry to a fine powder which is liable to blow away. And weeds love it!

Finally, avoid the worst mulch of all. Fresh grass clippings are deadly. Whole collections have been killed by mulching with clippings which heat up and kill the surface roots. If you use grass, make sure it is well composted and mixed with other things. Whichever mulch you choose, keep the layer thin. If you pile mulch on rhododendrons in thick layers, or layer upon layer, you bury the feeder roots and the plant will suffer.

Moving Rhododendrons

Because of their compact, fibrous rootballs, mature rhododendrons can generally be moved, even when they are very large, provided you can find the physical means to lift and move them. The British national rhododendron collection at Windsor Great Park was established by moving the huge collection from Tower Court. The majority of the plants, some of which were enormous, survived the move; many are still living quite happily.

We find that larger leaved species and hybrids are the easiest to move as large plants, dwarf rhododendrons move less well, and both evergreen and deciduous azaleas are often very slow to reestablish if moved as mature plants. The best time of year for such moving is generally in autumn, when rootballs are moist and the plants will have time to reestablish and then send out roots into the surrounding soil in spring before the heat of the summer. The exception to this is in very cold areas such as east North America where wind and frozen ground can easily desiccate newly planted specimens. Spring may be a better choice in such areas.

There are many reasons why a mature plant may need to be moved: the area may be crowded with too many plants close together, competing for light. The plant may be expanding to block a path. It may just look out of place with its surroundings. Often, as a rhododendron collector moves from hybrids to species, the massive colorful hybrids are given away to friends to be replaced with a connoisseur's selection of species.

Left: The garden soil is improved by the addition of organic matter such as conifer needles, leaf mold, and bark. These should be well mixed in.

Below: The famous peat beds at the Royal Botanic Garden, Edinburgh, constructed with peat blocks, are filled with dwarf rhododendrons, other dwarf Ericaceae, dwarf bulbs, and acid-loving perennials and alpines such as gentians.

When moving a rhododendron, try to keep as much width of rootball as possible since the most recent and most vigorous roots are usually at the outermost part of the rootball. Investigate with a spade until you find the healthy, new roots and dig around just outside this circle. The depth of rootball required is seldom much more than 1 ft. (30cm) and usually considerably less. Beware of trying to keep too much root as the weight of it (particularly when wet) may break the stem of the plant, or cause the whole root to drop off. If the rootball you end up with looks to be too small, because a bit breaks off for instance, or the foliage is sparse and straggly, it may be necessary to prune quite hard.

One of the easiest ways to move large plants is by making a sled out of heavy-duty polyethylene or similar material and simply dragging the plant along on this. Good soil preparation for the new hole, careful planting (see page 42) and diligent watering in the first growing season, are all crucial to good establishment.

Plants may need staking and artificial wind protection to prevent rocking and to allow quick anchoring from fresh roots put out into the surrounding soil.

Labeling

Many a fine collection has been reduced in value by inadequate labeling. While species can usually be identified, hybrids and azaleas are often very difficult and once the labels or records are lost, there is seldom a way back.

Over the years we have tried many different methods. Embossed labels, such as those found in botanical gardens, are clear, large, and last well but are very expensive. Probably the best cheap option we have tried are aluminum labels, written on in pencil. These are small and rather hard to find and they must be periodically loosened or relocated to avoid strangling the branch they are tied to. Plastic labels last only a few years and then become brittle. The writing of so-called indelible pens seems to last for only a year or two.

Whatever method you use, it is well worth keeping some sort of records of when and where things are planted. Such lists, and maps, have been invaluable to new owners of good collections. Do not forget to record collector's numbers on labels and in records.

Maintenance

Fertilizers and Feeding

Rhododendrons are not greedy plants when it comes to fertilizers; indeed, if you follow the correct procedures in soil preparation, with well-drained, moisture-retentive soil without competition from other plants, rhododendrons may need no feeding at all. Many fine collections, not to mention the plants in their wild state, get by without any application.

Vigor, good leaf retention, and deep green foliage are the signs of a healthy plant which needs no added help. Short growth, a sparse appearance, and pale or yellowish leaves all indicate an unhappy plant which may well require feeding, though the symptoms may also point to poor drainage or drought. The golden rule with rhododendrons is "little and often" rather than a single large dose. Most evergreen and deciduous azaleas and most larger hybrids can take considerable amounts of fertilizer without any ill effects and some, such as "Lem's Cameo" and some of its hybrids, seem to require extra large doses to maintain healthy foliage. Conversely, some dwarf varieties and many species are extremely sensitive and will suffer leaf tip burn or worse if you over do it. Young plants can be particularly sensitive.

Compound fertilizers contain three main ingredients: nitrogen, phosphorus, and potassium. These have an NPK rating giving the ratio of the three ingredients. For example 5N:5P:5K signifies equal amounts of each. Nitrogen is essential for growth and foliage formation and is quickly leached out of the soil, so needs to be replenished. It is this ingredient in excess which causes leaf scorch so it is important to be very careful with high-nitrogen fertilizers such as those used on vegetables. Phosphorus promotes root growth and the ripening of wood at the end of the season so the plant can withstand the winter. Potassium induces flower buds hardiness and disease resistance.

At Glendoick, we use a general fertilizer with a ratio 12N:6P:6K and sometimes add extra nitrogen using ammonium sulphate. Many fertilizers also contain trace elements which include calcium, sulphur, magnesium, iron, and other substances essential for healthy plant development. These minerals are required in minute quantities; too much of some of them can be as harmful as too little. The trace elements usually occur naturally in garden soils in sufficient quantity, and rarely need replenishing artificially, but they are useful for making potting composts for plants growing indoors and/or in containers.

Both organic and inorganic fertilizers can be used. Beware of farmyard manures; they can be extremely high in nitrogen if too fresh and can therefore cause severe leaf burn. This is especially true of poultry manure. Well-rotted cow manure is fine. Some of the substances used as mulches in parts of the world, such as pea straw and oilseed rape straw, are naturally high in nitrogen and will feed as they break down. Some of the traditional organic fertilizers such as bone meal are not particularly recommended for rhododendrons, though they are unlikely to do any harm.

Of the inorganic fertilizers, ammonium sulphate is undoubtedly the cheapest and most effective way to increase nitrogen in the soil. Yellow-leaved plants, if they are suffering from nitrogen deficiency due to the breakdown of organic materials in the compost, respond very quickly and soon green up. Use small doses at first and ensure that the powdery fertilizer is not left on the foliage, as it tends to burn. It can be washed off with water if it sticks to the leaves. Chlorosis (when leaves turn yellow with just the veins remaining green) can be caused by drainage problems, soil pH, or drought as well as by mineral deficiency. Iron chelates or sequestrols are often recommended as the cure-all for chlorotic foliage. This will only be of benefit if the problem is one of a lack of available iron. As the iron chelates are relatively expensive, try a small amount on a few plants during the growing season to see if there is any improvement. If lack of iron is the cause it should take no more than a month to green up the leaves.

How and when to feed

As the main feeder roots of a rhododendron are near the soil surface and tend to be at the perimeter of the rootball it is not usually worth putting fertilizer at the bottom of the hole (as recommended for many other plants). Nor is it worth scattering it around the trunks of older plants, as the feeder roots are further out. How much to put

Weeds

The shallow roots of rhododendrons are not good at competing with vigorous weeds for moisture. Hand weeding, hoeing, and weedkillers can be used but it is also worth looking at planting strategies that will reduce the need for weeding. In the wild, rhododendrons usually grow in colonies, growing into one another, providing shelter from wind and sun and preventing enough light reaching the ground for vigorous weeds to thrive. Often it is only moss that is found growing under dense canopies of rhododendrons in their native habitat. Particularly with dwarf and alpine rhododendrons, it is best to plant them in groups that will mat together and carpet the ground. Once this state begins to be achieved, the weeding required is minimal. Mulching is another method of reducing weed growth (see page 43). When hand-pulling weeds and hoeing, bear in mind that the shallow roots of rhododendrons are vulnerable to being exposed if soil is removed with the weed roots, or to being cut by careless hoeing.

on depends on the strength of the fertilizer and the composition and temperature of the soil. A soil whose organic content is mainly added bark or sawdust requires much more fertilizer than one which is predominantly peat or leaf mold.

Although some authorities recommend applying phosphate and potash outside the growing season, our own trials have shown no benefit from this. Wait until growth starts in spring and then feed with two to three small doses in the growing season. By midsummer, growth may be slowing down and flower buds are starting to be set. If you continue fertilizing beyond this time, it

tends to encourage leaves at the expense of flowering and makes the resultant soft growth vulnerable to early autumn frosts. This is especially important in severe climates, where new growth must have the maximum length of time to harden up before the onset of coldest midwinter temperatures.

For young plants, such as recently propagated material, as well as plants

Slow-release fertilizer pellets are incorporated into the compost of container-grown plants and provide nutrients and trace elements for up to 18 months.

grown in pots or other containers, slow-release granules or liquid feeding to the roots or foliage are often the safest and most convenient methods. Slow-release granules can last up to 18 months and can be incorporated into the potting mix. These usually contain all three major ingredients as well as trace elements. Liquid foliar feeding is another excellent method, as the little and often philosophy allows careful monitoring of any signs of leaf tip burn caused by too much nitrogen. Liquid feeding mature plants outdoors is also possible.

Herbicides and Weedkillers

Weedkillers are either total or selective (that is they will kill everything or only specific plants). Their action is contact (surface only) or systemic (penetrate the plant itself) or preemergence (kills germinating seedlings). All have their place in rhododendron growing, but environmental concerns should always be borne in mind before using them. Legislation concerning their use by professional growers and amateurs varies greatly from country to country and rules are constantly changing, so I have not been specific here.

All weedkillers are, of course, potentially dangerous, harmful to humans and wildlife, and they can pollute water. Many should be used with protective clothing and some have very unpleasant fumes. Spray must be fine to coat leaves effectively, which means that spraying should be done on fairly calm days. Wetting agents can be added to some chemicals to increase their effectiveness. Some herbicides, such as glyphosate require a minimum dry period to work well. Some of the preemergence weedkillers are relatively safe to apply as they come in granular form and can be applied with a "pepper-pot" type shaker, which ensures even distribution.

Total weedkillers are used to clean up an area before planting. Glyphosate is now the most common total weedkiller used by professionals and amateurs, replacing the much more dangerous sodium-chlorate. Effective by systemic action on most herbaceous weeds and some woody ones, including *R. ponticum*, it should be used when weeds are in full growth. The foliage of stubborn weeds with a waxy leaf surface, such as ivy, may need to be bruised before application. Planting of the area can commence seven days after application as it is not residual in the soil. The hormone weedkiller 2,4,D is effective on hard-to-eradicate weeds such as creeping thistle. Triclopyr can be used in grassland, but is not safe to use around cultivated rhododendrons. It is very effective for stubborn woody weeds such as tree saplings, brambles (*Rubus*), *R. ponticum*, broom and others such as nettles.

Selective weedkillers. Developed for use against difficult-to-eradicate weeds, destroying one plant growing among other sorts, e.g., broadleaved weeds in grass. One of the best is cycloxydim which kills grass (including couch) but which is virtually harmless to most other cultivated plants, so may be sprayed among them. Asulam is invaluable for killing bracken and docks (Rumex) and we have used it successfully around mature plants in our Argyll garden without adverse effects.

Contact Weedkillers such as paraquat and diquat. These quickly kill the top growth of most weeds but are inactivate in the soil. These chemicals are usually harmless on woody trunks so can be used right up to old, established rhododendrons. Damage occurs to anything green, including leaves and any stems and trunks that remain green from chlorophyll. Maples are an example. Drift causes unsightly black spotting on rhododendron foliage. Both can even be applied during rain. They encourage the growth of moss and are sometimes used deliberately for this purpose. These very useful products may be removed from the market due to environmental concerns. An alternative is the gas flame-gun which, rather than actually burning the weeds, causes fatal damage to plant cells. Obviously extreme care should be taken to avoid damaging precious plants.

Preemergence weedkillers are applied to clean soil and kill germinating seed. They can be watered or sprinkled around growing plants. They generally have little effect on established weeds, so they are best applied after an area has been cleaned by other means. Some of them have been proven to cause damage to rhododendrons. There are some rhododendron varieties that are sensitive to them, especially as young plants. We have found that specific weeds, such as nettles and cleavers (*Galium*) are resistant to certain preemergence herbicides. It is advisable to wash the foliage of rhododendrons after applying, in case there are any adverse effects.

Pinching and Pruning

It is another of the old myths about rhododendron cultivation that you cannot, or should not, pinch and prune them to improve their shape. Despite the fact that many of the books on the subject say pruning is not necessary, nurserymen do it constantly to produce those symmetrical bushes that garden centers like to

stock and their customers like to buy. As far as improving the shape of rhododendrons, pinching is preventative while pruning is a cure. Pinching means removing the terminal or central growth bud of a rhododendron shoot as it elongates, in order to encourage multiple branching lower down. Pruning involves cutting a shoot or branch so that buds break further down, hopefully improving the shape.

I am not claiming that rhododendrons require pruning in the same way that a rose, for instance, does on an annual basis. It is just a tool that can be used from time to time to improve the shape of your

Pinching

Removing the central growth bud (right) encourages branching below as can be seen on the left where three growth buds are starting to swell. Each will produce a new shoot, encouraging bushiness.

plants. Many of the alpine and dwarf varieties such as "yak" hybrids need little or no pruning to maintain a good shape, as long as they are grown in plenty of light. As soon as rhododendrons start to flower freely, most growth comes from lateral shoots below the flower buds and, therefore, nature does its own pinching.

When plants are young and before they start to flower freely, the simplest way to ensure a plant of good habit is to pinch out all the single, terminal buds as they elongate in the spring. Wait until this becomes easy to do: If you have to dig out the bud, it is too early. I recommend this for vigorous dwarfs, subsection Triflora species, and most larger hybrids.

With species, many of the largest ones are, in essence, trees and they should be left to form a single trunk until they reach a good height. Others, such as the very vigorous *R. decorum*, are better pinched as a small plant to encourage bushiness. Spring frosts do a lot of natural pinching, with the central bud being frosted and leaving the later growth to come from below as multiple shoots. This usually gives good results, though I have seen some large-leaved species that were frosted so often that their growth became unnaturally congested.

There are several reasons why you may want to prune a bush. It may have become crowded out by other plants and have

become straggly. It may have been severely damaged by cold or wind, or had its first flush of growth frosted, causing unsightly, brown, distorted foliage. You may want to reduce it in size because it has got too big or because you want to move it. Perhaps the most common pruning tasks are when you want to rejuvenate an old collection that has become completely overgrown.

Scaly leaved rhododendrons and all azaleas can be pruned to any point on a branch or shoot and new growth will come from buds lower down. With larger-leaved non-scaly varieties, you must cut back to a whorl of leaves (see photo). New growth will only come from a bud, or buds, within these leaves.

Although it is possible to prune at any time of year, perhaps the most satisfactory time is straight after flowering (except for varieties flowering later than early summer). This gives time for production of new growth and, hopefully, formation of flower buds for the following year. Alternatively, prune in early spring, before new growth is starting to elongate.

When pruning larger-leaved varieties, cut back to just above a circle of leaves (known as a whorl). Even if the old leaves have dropped off, it should be possible to see where a whorl of leaves was and cut back to this point.

Scaly leaved rhododendrons and almost all azaleas can be pruned with success. Azaleas and species from subsection Triflora such as *R. yunnanense* and *R. augustinii* can be hard pruned and, provided the roots are healthy, they soon send out plenty of new growth. Most small-leaved dwarfs can be pruned into shape, but it is best to leave a fair amount of leaves: cutting back into too much old wood is risky. Maddenia and Vireyas grown indoors tend to get straggly if not hard pruned every few years. Among larger species and hybrids, there is considerable variation in how well they respond. If you can cut back to a healthy whorl of leaves, one or some of the buds above each leaf stalk will almost certainly grow.

It is when a more severe pruning is required, cutting back to a bare trunk, that results vary considerably. As a general rule, those with a smooth bark such as *R. thomsonii*, *R. barbatum*, and some of the large-leaved species such as *R. sinogrande* are reluctant to respond to this. Of the large-leaved species, *R. macabeanum* can produce plenty of shoots out from the base if cut back deliberately or by severe weather.

Among the best responders are *R. arboreum* and the ubiquitous *R. ponticum*. The latter's ability to regenerate is one of the reasons it is so hard to eradicate in areas where it has become a pest. This species was traditionally used as a rootstock for grafting cultivars and its extreme propensity to throw suckers has in many cases meant that the rootstock has overwhelmed whatever was grafted on top of it. This is important to bear in mind when trying to rejuvenate bushes that date back to the 1950s or earlier.

The characteristic dark green, shiny, narrow leaves of *R. ponticum* should make it possible to identify, even outside flowering time, which stems are suckers. Suckers should be broken off at the base of the stem. If you prune them off, they will just produce a whole cluster of shoots from below the cut.

Since the 1950s, cuttings, and more recently, micropropagation have been the major production techniques for rhododendrons (except in northern Europe where most cultivars are grafted on "Cunningham's White," which fortunately is far less prone to suckering).

Dead-heading

Rhododendrons are not perpetual-flowering so dead-heading does not prolong the flowering season as it does with some rose varieties, for instance. There are, however, sound arguments for doing at least some deadheading. Rhododendrons are a rather promiscuous lot and they are very often cross-pollinated by insects. The resulting seed set can be large and unsightly but, more importantly, it waste energy in ripening seed, discouraging vigorous new growth and, therefore, a good flowering season the following year. If you only have a few rhododen-

Deadheading

1. Firmly grasp the base of the truss (after the flowers have fallen off).

2. Snap the flower stem off at the base as cleanly as possible, being careful not to damage the emerging buds below.

1

2

drons, deadhead them if you have time. If you have a large collection, then concentrate on those which will benefit the most. Young plants, especially those bought and planted in flower, will definitely benefit. So will most larger-growing species that produce enormous, multiple-flowered trusses. Anything with a mass of swelling seed heads is best deadheaded.

Most popular hardy hybrids, "yak" hybrids, dwarfs, and deciduous and evergreen azaleas seldom need it and will flower well every year whether deadheaded or not. One or two dwarfs such as *R. campylogynum* tend to produce large, unsightly seed heads held above the foliage, which are most easily removed with a pair of scissors. The technique when removing spent flower heads from larger species and hybrids is to break the truss off at the base above the whorl of leaves below it. Be careful not to break off the emerging growth buds underneath. Take your time until you get the knack; it does not take long before you can do it very quickly.

Irrigation and Watering

On the mountains of the Himalayas and China, there is typically a relatively dry period in spring when flowering occurs, and this is followed by heavy monsoon rains during the main part of the growing season. Few of us are fortunate (or unfortunate!) enough to live in areas with such reliable summer rains, so we are forced to supplement our rainfall with artificial watering.

Rhododendron root systems are shallow and compact, so if the soil dries out, they are one of the first plants to wilt. None will withstand sustained periods of drought, but small-leaved species and evergreen azaleas plus one or two larger-leaved species, such as *R. macrophyllum* and *R. decorum*, are able to tolerate fairly dry conditions. Ample moisture throughout the growing season is required to see the spectacular large leaves on species such as *R. sinogrande*. Rhododendrons wilt and curl up their leaves very demonstratively when they are suffering from lack of water. Most varieties can withstand this for a few days without ill effects but, if it happens when there is new growth unfurling, this tends to stunt its size.

Watering systems vary hugely, from a single can or hose for a small garden, to sophisticated and computer-controlled sprinkler systems with pipes buried underground. Seep-hose and trickle irrigation, which slowly leak water from numerous holes or small pipes laid in or on the planting beds, are an excellent way of directing moisture to exactly where it is needed, and cut down on waste. As a general rule it is better to give plants an occasional good soaking than a series of inadequate doses. Rhododendrons with good root systems can survive a

surprising amount of drought, though the stress this incurs may make them vulnerable to other problems such as honey fungus. In very hot weather it is best to water in early morning or late at night to avoid burning of foliage and evaporation. Excess water coupled with poor drainage and high temperature is a sure recipe for the lethal *Phytophthora* root rot. Watering plants in flower in warm climates encourages petal blight, which can soon ruin the flowers completely.

With recent changes in weather patterns, as well as huge increases in demand, water is becoming a precious commodity and the threat of rationing hangs over many gardens. There are various things that can be done to cut down on the amount of watering required. Autumn planting with plenty of moisture-retaining organic matter and good mulching are well worth considering.

In our experience, tree roots rather than evaporation are the most common cause of dry soil. If greedy trees cannot be removed or are required for shade and shelter, it may be worth trying to isolate the rhododendron roots from the tree roots with barriers such as thick polyethylene. We have found that beds lined with polyethylene (ensuring good drainage) with a good mulch almost never require watering, even in our sunny garden with long periods of inadequate rain. In areas with alkaline soil, this method

may be essential, as all watering will have to be done with collected rainwater. The fact that seep-hoses and trickle hoses can be buried means they are much less wasteful and, they should be encouraged in any case.

There are several advantages to cutting down watering in late summer, even to the extent of causing some stress to the plants. In very severe climates, where fully ripened wood is essential to withstand extreme lows of temperature, plants that go on growing into the autumn are very vulnerable to damage. Those whose roots are allowed to dry out from late summer onward are much better prepared for winter. It is, however, important to water the plants thoroughly in autumn, if conditions are dry, before the onset of winter.

In all climates, cutting down on watering in late summer encourages the setting of flower buds for next season; nurserymen do this as a matter of course.

Propagation

POLLINATING A FLOWER

Fig. 1

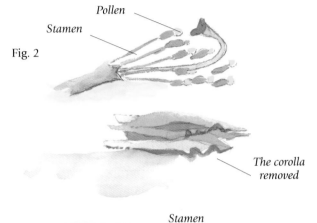

Fig. 2

Flower bud

Pollen

Stamen

The corolla removed

Stamen

Fig. 3

Pollen

Stigma

Fig. 1: The unopened flower bud, a day or two before opening.

Fig. 2: The unopened corolla is removed, revealing the stigma and and stamens. The stamens should be removed at this point.

Fig. 3: Several days later, the stigma becomes ripe (sticky) and the pollen of the male parent can applied.

Below: A cross-section of a flower, showing the floral parts.

Rhododendrons and azaleas are not one of the easier plant groups to propagate; seedlings are slow-growing and cuttings generally take several months to root. With a little care and attention, however, it is possible to have very successful results.

Propagation falls into two main categories, sexual (from seed) or asexual (cuttings, layers, grafts, etc.). The crucial difference is that from sexual reproduction, the offspring are all different and are NOT identical to the parent, while the asexual, or vegetative, methods produce plants that are an exact replica of the parent. All named varieties and selected clones must be produced by vegetative means.

Seed

This method can be used to raise species from wild or garden seed and for creating new hybrids. It cannot be used to reproduce a named hybrid. Seeds grown from "Pink Pearl" are not "Pink Pearl."

Rhododendrons are notoriously promiscuous; this means that in a garden they will be cross-pollinated by insects flying from one plant to another and the seed-grown offspring will almost always be hybridized, unless there is no compatible plant flowering at the same time in the vicinity.

If you want to grow species or make hybrids from garden seed, you have to make deliberately controlled pollinations. This involves removing the corolla (petals) and stamens from the flower on the female parent before it

PARTS OF A FLOWER

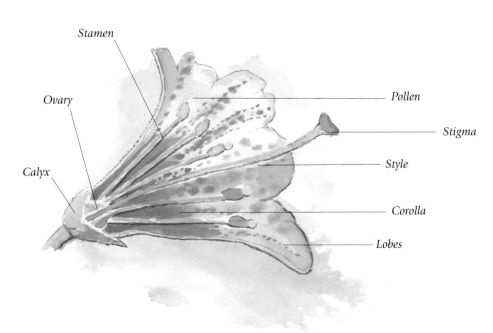

Stamen

Ovary

Calyx

Pollen

Stigma

Style

Corolla

Lobes

1

opens, waiting for the stigma to ripen (it becomes sticky), and then applying pollen from the stamens of the other (male) parent to the ripened stigma. Pollen can be stored in a fridge for several weeks; it also can be frozen and thawed and sent through the mail, so the male parent does not have to be flowering nearby or at the same time.

Do not forget to label the pollinated flower and record it so you can find the right seed capsules in the autumn. Seed of both hybrids and species is available from

Rhododendron Society seed exchanges. The most exciting seed to grow is that collected in the wild. Such seed often has a collector's number recording by whom, when, and where the seed was collected.

Rhododendron seed takes three to seven months to ripen and is therefore harvested in the autumn or winter following pollination. The seed capsules will be swollen and turning brown. Try to collect them just before they split. If capsules are collected green, place them in a dry place such as a window sill and they will dry and split within a few days or weeks.

Hybridization

1. The pollen from the stamens of the male parent is applied to the stigmas of the emasculated female parent. The stigma is ready for pollination when it is sticky.

2. The ovary starting to swell after a successful pollination. The smaller ovaries have not been successfully pollinated.

The seed is fairly small. Try to separate the seed from the chaff and debris to prevent mold. Once dried, it can be stored in envelopes in the fridge until you are ready to sow. Seed should be sown in pans or trays containing moist (but not soaking) peat or clean, live sphagnum moss. Sow seed thinly onto the surface and do not cover with compost. We find covering pans with perforated polyethylene keeps the humidity up but lets air circulate.

Germination usually takes two to three weeks if the temperature is 15–20°F (59–70°C) in a propagator or heated frame.

In a cold frame, germination will probably not take place until the spring. All watering of seed pans should be done by soaking from below to avoid encouraging mold on the foliage. Once seed has germinated it needs sufficient

57

light (but not direct sunlight) to keep plants strong and compact. Inadequate light causes weak etiolated (drawn) seedlings.

When large enough to handle, transplant the seedlings into trays in a peat-based compost. Be very careful with feeding at this stage as seedlings, especially dwarfs and species, are very sensitive to fertilizer. Use slow-release or dilute liquid feed. Usually, seedlings are best over-wintered under cover, in a cold frame, greenhouse or similar. Small seedlings are vulnerable to botrytis (mold) and other pests and diseases (see page 66).

Asexual/ Clonal Methods

LAYERING

This is a good method to obtain a few new plants. It involves bending side branches of the chosen plant into the surrounding soil so that they make roots. In moist climates, it often happens naturally. After one to three years (depending on the variety, soil penetration, and rainfall), the rooted, layered shoot can be cut from the mother plant and moved elsewhere.

Above: Ripened and splitting seed capsules collected in the autumn, showing the chambers filled with seeds. The seeds are relatively large, indicating a larger-growing variety.

Right: Seedlings in a seed pan. These are becoming rather crowded and will soon need to be transplanted.

Left: Sowing seeds on the surface of a seed pan. Try to sow the seeds fairly thinly to avoid overcrowding when the seedlings germinate.

Right: Seedlings transplanted into a seed tray in a peat-based compost.

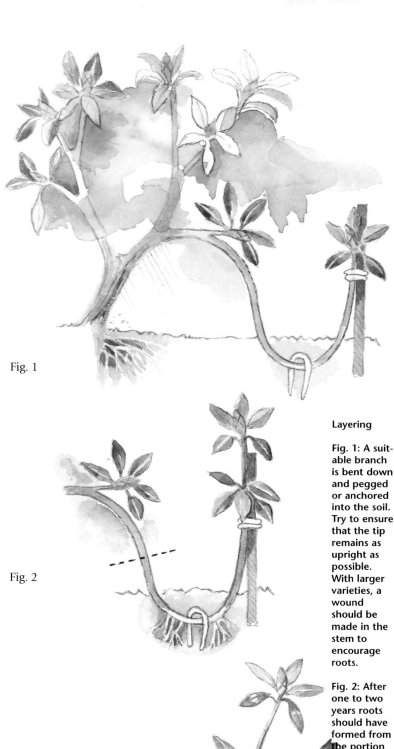

Fig. 1

Fig. 2

Fig. 3

Layering

Fig. 1: A suitable branch is bent down and pegged or anchored into the soil. Try to ensure that the tip remains as upright as possible. With larger varieties, a wound should be made in the stem to encourage roots.

Fig. 2: After one to two years roots should have formed from the portion of the branch that has been buried in the ground. The layer can then be severed from the mother plant.

Fig. 3: The layer is now ready for transplanting.

Varieties that are very upright in habit are unlikely to have suitable branches to layer. It is usually advisable to improve the soil (where the layers will be made) by adding organic matter. In moist climates, you can layer into pots or trays placed around the growing plant, which avoids root disturbance when the layers are cut.

With dwarf varieties, shoots can be anchored using rocks and stones. With larger varieties, layers are usually held in place with stakes, or wire. Bend the branch or shoot into the surrounding (prepared if necessary) soil and anchor it so that the end of the shoot is as near upright as possible. Many layers can be made from a single specimen, we have sometimes layered the entire plant.

To encourage root production in larger varieties it is advisable to cut a thin layer of bark off the underside of the branch or shoot where it is to be anchored into the ground. Once a good root system has formed, the plant can be severed from the mother and transplanted. Ensure the layers are well watered before moving them. The disadvantage of layered plants is that they usually have a rather obvious bend in the stem. Judicious pruning can usually result in an acceptable specimen.

CUTTINGS

Rhododendrons and azaleas vary greatly in the ease with which they root from cuttings. Evergreen azaleas and most dwarf rhododendrons are relatively easy, while many species, deciduous azaleas and larger hybrids, are rather slow and tricky to root. One or two varieties refuse point-blank to root at all, and these have to be grafted.

The easiest way to root rhododendrons is under polyethylene in a box, tray, pots, or modules, or in a propagator; ensure these are all well cleaned before use. Some people have small mist systems that can give excellent results, but which require more looking after. Bottom heat is advisable but not essential; without it, cuttings put in during late summer or autumn will take twice or three times as long to root. Cuttings should be taken when they are sufficiently hardened up to be flexible and springy when subjected to a bit of bending. This tends to be from late summer onward.

Dwarfs and evergreen azaleas should be cut to 1–2 in. (2.5–5cm) or so, larger varieties can be up to 4 in. (10cm) long. Remove leaves to form a single circle of four to seven leaves at the top of a cutting. Shaded leaves tend to rot in the rooting bed. With longer-leaved varieties, you can reduce the leaf length by 30–40 percent to save space. The most satisfactory rooting media tend to be 50–60 percent peat and 40–50 percent composted bark, perlite, sand, or other substance to keep the compost open. Rooting hormones are useful to speed up the process.

With larger varieties it also helps to cut a thin slice off the lower stem. Compost should be moist but not wet, as this causes rotting. Cuttings can be sprayed with a general fungicide to discourage disease. Cover them with a propagator lid, polyethylene sheet, or a polyethylene bag, making it more or less airtight so that the humidity is maintained.

Keeping the atmosphere humid is most important. If the leaves dry out, the cuttings wilt and will not root. They need plenty of light but must be shaded from direct sunlight. Cuttings root best with bottom heat of 59–70°F (15–20°C). In mid-winter we reduce heat to about 50°F (10°C), as light levels are very low.

Check over the cuttings regularly and remove any dead material to avoid the spread of disease. Once roots have formed that are roughly the same size as the foliage on the cutting, it should be removed from the heat and hardened off by covering it with slit polyethylene, or material shading.

Rooted cuttings can be transplanted into a peat-based compost that will usually also contain some composted bark, perlite, leaf mold, or needles, and often some slow-release fertilizer. Some protection will be needed for most of their first growing season. We transplant our cuttings outside at the end of their first growing season. Beware of vine weevil in pots and trays (see page 64).

The other propagation methods, grafting and tissue culture, tend to be for professionals and avid amateurs only. Consult the further reading list for sources of information on these methods (see page 124).

Top left: In preparing cuttings, remove large flower buds, trim the leaves if they are long. With thicker-stemmed varieties, make a thin cut or "wound" on the lower portion of the stem.

Center left: The clearly labeled cuttings are covered with thin transparent polyethylene, placed directly on, or held up just above the cuttings.

Opposite: Place cuttings in a tray, spacing them so that leaves do not overlap too much. Overcrowding encourages rotting.

Bottom left: Cuttings showing root development. The roots are just starting to grow on the cutting on the right. The cutting on the left has a rootball large enough to remove from the rooting tray or bench and it will now be hardened off.

Pests and Diseases

Although the list of pests and diseases in this section is quite daunting, you will be relieved to know that each area where rhododendrons are grown suffers only some of them. Indeed it is possible to say that in areas with a moderate climate, the most likely-to-be-encountered pest will be vine weevil, the most damaging disease powdery mildew, and the most irksome climatic problem spring frosts. Many of the other problems are unlikely to be encountered. On the other hand, where temperatures are more extreme, such as in eastern North America and parts of continental Europe, the problems are more likely to include stem and root rots, and others associated with these climates such as winter cold damage. More plants are killed or maimed by poor soil preparation and lack of care in the first growing season than most of the other problems put together.

Pests

WARM-BLOODED PESTS

Rhododendrons are poisonous to many animals, which usually know not to eat them, but there are cases of sheep and cattle poisoning from time to time. Horses and cattle are more likely to cause breakage than to graze your plants, but this and the soil compaction that they can cause means that is advisable to keep farm animals fenced from your rhododendrons. Birds can cause considerable damage, both in dust bathing and in looking for food, especially around small, newly planted stock. Indoors and in frames, mice and voles can be troublesome, especially in cold and snowy winters.

Two common animal pests are deer and rabbits. Both tend to be rather particular as to which varieties or groups of varieties they prefer to eat. Azaleas, both deciduous and evergreen, seem to be especially palatable, and certain species such as *R. canadense* always seem to be the first to be attacked. When grazing is lush and there is plenty to eat, rhododendrons are often left alone. The problems usually occur when there is snow on the ground, especially when the earth is frozen solid. Often, rhododendrons are one of the few evergreen plants that deer and rabbits can easily reach and so considerable damage, such as the loss of leaf tips, branch tips or, more seriously, the stripping of the bark, may occur.

Ideally, fencing is the perfect option, but this is expensive, especially where deer are concerned. To fence effectively against rabbits, use netting at least 3 ft. (1m) wide and bury 4–6 in. (10–15cm) in the ground to prevent them from digging underneath. An effective deer fence needs to be a minimum of 6 ft. (2m) high but may need to be higher, depending upon the species of deer.

Right: A plant that has had the bark eaten off around the base by vine weevil larvae, completely girdling the stem. This is almost always fatal, though collapse may take several months.

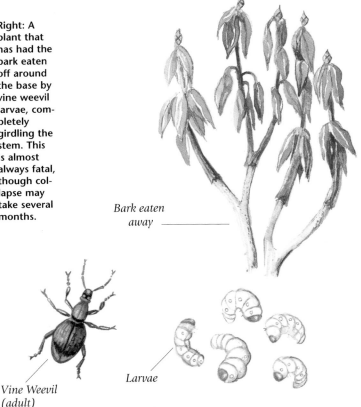

Bark eaten away —————

Vine Weevil (adult)

Larvae

Above left: The adult vine weevil (2x life size) is usually around ½ in. (1cm) long and cuts notches out of rhododendron leaves at night.

Above right: The very destructive vine weevil grubs eat the roots and bark of rhododendrons and many other plants and can often be fatal. They are quite hard to control.

The alternative is to attempt to protect vulnerable plants with substances whose smell will discourage the deer. Some people swear by bundles of human hair (try your local hairdresser), while others obtain dung of predatory animals such as lions from their local zoo! Several commercial animal repellents have been developed over the years. The most common is aluminium ammonium sulphate (sold under the name 'scoot', 'stay off', etc). A substance called Bitrex is now available in North America. This is taken up by the plant, making its leaves unpalatable to all animals.

INSECT PESTS

Vine Weevil

Black vine weevil (and possibly other closely related species) is probably the most serious pest that affects rhododendrons. Its incidence is on the increase and it is notoriously difficult to control, especially for the amateur grower. The damage by vine weevil falls into two categories: that caused to foliage by adults, and the more serious damage caused underground by larvae. The adult vine weevil is a flightless black beetle about ½ in. (1cm) long, which is seldom seen as it feeds at night. It eats irregular notches in the margins of leaves (unlike caterpillars, which usually eat away whole portions of the leaf or make holes in it). This damage is seldom more than cosmetic and it often tends to occur in shady conditions where the insects can shelter in the undergrowth or leaf litter during the day. A plant moved out into more light will often not be attacked. Alternatively, a plant can be sprayed with a contact insecticide. In North America, the most popular chemical is acephate (most commonly sold under the name Orthene) which is both contact and systemic, i.e. it kills insects it touches and it enters the leaves, rendering them poisonous when eaten (but apparently only for a period of three days). Contact insecticides such as fenitrothion, malathion (which kill by spraying the insect itself) are of limited use unless you are prepared to get up in the middle of the night to spray the feeding weevils.

Adults tend to hatch out from late spring onward and need to feed for several weeks before egg-laying can begin; the main reason to kill adults is to prevent them from laying the eggs that produce the much more damaging larvae. Each adult can lay several hundreds of eggs and one larva can kill a young plant on its own, especially if it is in a container. Spray the foliage of plants as soon as the characteristic notching is seen on the new growth of the rhododendron.

The vine weevil larvae are white, "C" or crescent shaped, ½ in. (1-1.2cm) long at maturity with a brownish head. They hatch out from eggs laid around the stem of plants

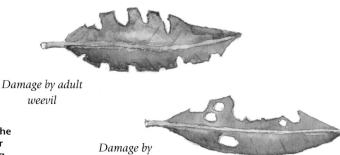

Damage by adult weevil

Damage by caterpillar

Right: The irregular notching typical of adult vine weevil (top) on a rhododendron leaf in contrast to the more general damage done by caterpillars (bottom).

Below: Irregular notching on the leaf margins is usually caused by adult vine weevils which feed at night.

(usually in summer or autumn) and eat either the bark or the roots of the plant through late summer, autumn, and winter. The girdling of the bark all round the stem at soil level, or above and below it, usually results in death, the plant collapsing quite quickly during the growing season but more slowly during the winter. This is the most common damage in containers. In the open ground, the larvae tend to graze the fresh roots. On an older plant, this is often more debilitating than fatal unless there are large numbers of larvae, but in small and young plants, the root eating can cause death.

Many plants are very vulnerable to vine weevil. Some of their favorites include young yew, strawberries, and primulas. Some people use such plants as indicators to show when weevils are active. For amateurs, apart from targeting adults with insecticides, the main weapons available are biological controls against larvae. These include nematode (eelworm) species *Steinernema* and *Heterorhabditis*. These products are available by mail order and arrive in a packet, the contents of

which are mixed with lukewarm water in a watering can and watered on. Nematodes (eelworms) require a minimum temperature to breed and attack the weevil larvae and so are only effective in warm weather outdoors. They are most useful in greenhouses and in containers, where the worst problems occur. Compost must be moist so that the nematode solution can soak well into the soil. The best time to apply is mid to late summer when soil temperatures are high and before larvae have had a chance to do too much damage. The fact that weevils are flightless means that infestations usually start in localized areas and, provided these can be dealt with, the spread may be halted. A promising recent development is the insecticide imidacloprid which is now available to amateurs. It is incorporated into compost and protects the roots and leaves from vine weevil and other insects, including aphids, for up to one year.

Aphids

Whitefly and greenfly can suddenly appear in large number on the underside of young leaves and on the stems, particularly in dry weather, sucking out the sap and causing puckered or wrinkled leaves. Vireyas seem particularly prone to attack.

Spray with a systemic insecticide. If you dislike using chemicals, soap concentrates can be used. It may take several doses to clear the infestation. With both chemicals and soap sprays, it is important to target the insects on the leaf undersides. This requires a fine spray to allow the water droplets to adhere. There are also a number of biological controls that are most effective under glass. These include *Aphidoletes* (midge) and *Aphidius* (predatory wasp).

Other Insect Pests

Caterpillars (from several species of moth, depending on the part of the world) can be troublesome and we find that they do most damage to certain plants where the caterpillars drop from surrounding trees and shrubs. Sometimes they destroy expanding buds, leaving shredded new growth that usually has to be removed. If you cannot pick off and squash the offenders by hand, then use a suitable chemical control. Other insect pests can be very troublesome locally or regionally, but are not widespread.

Scale is a small insect that sucks sap and leaves an unsightly black residue of sooty mold. Spray with insecticide and to kill adults in winter, spray with an oil spray or oil plus malathion or diazinon.

Thrips are a problem in warm and dry climates such as California and parts of New Zealand. Thrips are characterized by a silvery discoloration on the leaf's upper surface. Most of the standard insecticides and insecticidal soaps can be used. Locally, biological controls may also be available.

Other pests such as red spider mites, capsid bugs (a.k.a. plant or leaf bugs), rhododendron borer, lacewing, and leaf miners can cause damage locally. All can be treated with suitable chemicals if necessary.

Diseases

POWDERY MILDEW

Mildews occur on many plant genera with new strains and mutations occurring from time to time.

There are three different powdery mildews that attack the genus *Rhododendron*. The three types appear to be mutually exclusive as regards the parts of the genus they affect. One mildew occurs on deciduous azaleas, one on Vireyas, and the most troublesome occurs on temperate rhododendron (as opposed to azalea) species and hybrids.

Powdery mildew showing the typical patches of powdery mycelium on the leaf's lower surface. These can vary in color from grayish to brown or fawn.

Deciduous Azalea Mildew

Characterized by a silvery mycelium that develops on the upper and sometimes lower surface of the leaf from midsummer onward. It occurs on wild populations of *R. occidentale* in western North America and on cultivated azaleas, particularly varieties containing *R. occidentale* and *R. luteum*, which includes many of the paler-flowered and scented ones. Most azalea species and hybrids with orange and red flowers seem to be resistant. Apart from being unsightly, the disease, if unchecked, can cause early leaf fall and therefore a general loss of

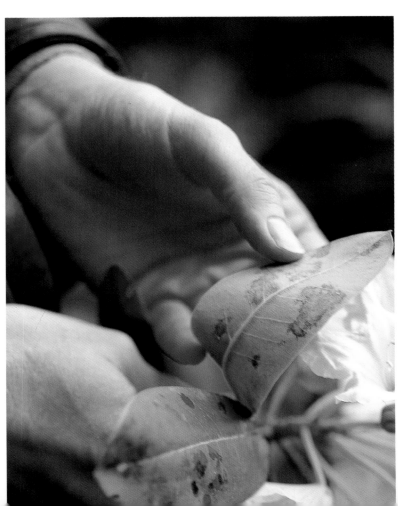

Mildew-Susceptible Plants

Species: *R. cinnabarinum*, *R. thomsonii*, and their relatives, *R. calostrotum* ssp. *riparioides*.

Hybrids: most *R. cinnabarinum* hybrids such as "Lady Chamberlain" and "Lady Rosebery," *R. thomsonii* hybrids, e.g., "Cornish Cross," "Naomi, *R. griersonianum* hybrids such as "Vanessa Pastel," "Anna Rose Whitney," "Elizabeth" and yellow hybrids containing *R. wardii* such as "Virginia Richards," " Lila Pedigo," "Golden Star" etc. Semidwarfs such as "Seta."

The only sure way to control this disease is to spray with suitable systemic fungicides, but this only works as a preventative and only for as long as you spray. I know of no effective nonchemical or organic controls, though several avenues are being pursued.

Only recently developed growth is susceptible to the disease. It will not spread onto old leaves. New growth should therefore be sprayed as soon as it is fully extended. This will probably be from late spring to mid-summer in the northern hemisphere. The problem is that many smaller-leaved plants produce new growth more or less continuously through the growing season, and this requires a spraying program every 3-4 weeks from late spring to autumn. The disease spreads most quickly in

vigor and decrease in flowering. Breeding for mildew resistance has been quite successful and many disease-resistant cultivars are available. For susceptible cultivars, spray with a suitable fungicide. This strain of mildew has recently spread to Europe.

Vireya Mildew

This is apparently a mildew that also affects other parts of the family Ericaceae such as *Gaultheria*. It is characterized by white patches on the young leaves that often become under-sized or distorted. It can be controlled using the same fungicides as are used to treat rhododendron mildew.

Rhododendron Powdery Mildew

Although said to have been first reported in the 1960s, this disease did not start to cause problems until the early 1980s. Since then, it has become one of the major problems for rhododendron growers in moderate climates such as the British Isles, western North America, Australia, and New Zealand. In places with high summer temperatures and/or cold winters, such as most of Germany, Sweden, and Eastern North America (except the most favorable coastal areas), it has not become widespread.

Powdery mildew showing typical discoloration on the upper surface of the leaf.

The symptoms are light, usually yellowish rings, circles or blotches on the upper leaf, which correspond on the leaf's lower surface with brown or grey patches of mycelium. These may spread and cover the whole surface or just remain as patches. Severe infections cause premature leaf-drop and a plant can be defoliated. Unless the subsequent new growth is kept clear of the disease, the plant cannot photosynthesize and may die. Thankfully, only some species and cultivars are susceptible to the problem though, if the infection is allowed to increase unchecked, most varieties can be affected to some extent.

dry, mild weather and in conditions of shade and of poor air circulation. Over-planted or mature, dense gardens are therefore often the worst affected and, of course, large plants are the hardest and most time-consuming to spray.

There are several possible strategies to follow in dealing with this disease: **Option 1** Spray all your plants several times a year. Using large amounts of fungicide is a dangerous, unpleasant, time-consuming and expensive business. It is possible, however, to keep everything disease-free.
Option 2 Identify and spray only the most susceptible plants. This should prevent obvious sources of infection building up in the garden and it may well cut down infection to other plants. Those plants that can live happily with moderate levels of infection can be left to fend for themselves.
Option 3 Let nature take its course. You will probably lose the most susceptible plants such as "Lady Chamberlain" and "Elizabeth" and badly infected plants are always a source of infection. Some will look semipermanently under-clothed and sparse with unsightly disease. It may be worth eliminating these as a preventative measure and avoiding susceptible ones when planting. Several gardens have chosen or been forced to take this course. Although some plants have been lost, the effect of the disease on the majority is largely cosmetic and most

flower and grow freely. We have never sprayed in our garden and have only lost a few *R. cinnabarinum* from the disease.

Rust
Like the mildews, rusts are a group of constantly evolving fungi that attack many genera of plants. In wild populations, rusts are most commonly found on natural hybrids. There are several species of rust (up to 13 have been reported) that attack rhododendrons in different parts of the world and that have differing alternative hosts. (Most rusts have two hosts, and the rust moves from one host to the other as part of its life cycle, though apparently it can live for several years on one host.)

Rhododendron rusts have alternative hosts, which include *Picea* and *Tsuga*. Rust usually appears on the leaf underside and is characterized by the spores that form an orange powdery covering. If left untreated, it will cause black spotting on the upper surface of the leaf and infected leaves will usually drop off. As with mildew, a severe attack can defoliate and kill a plant, though this is rare except in the most susceptible varieties. Many of the mildew fungicides are also effective on rusts.

Rust-Susceptible Plants:
Few species are very susceptible.
Hybrids: *R cinnabarinum* hybrids such as "Trewithen Orange," *R. edgeworthii* hybrids such as

"Fragrantissimum." Azaleodendrons such as "Martha Isaacson." Dwarf hybrids such as "Anna Baldsiefen" and "Arctic Tern."

Rusts seem to be affecting more varieties and cultivars from year to year.

Above: Rust on rhodo-dendrons is characterized by black or dark brown spotting on the upper leaf surface which, at certain times of year, is matched by orange spores on the lower leaf surface.

Right: The healthy white roots of the left hand plant contrast with the dark brown dead ones of a plant killed by root rot.

Root Rot and Stem Dieback
In hot climates, these diseases are undoubtedly the greatest causes of rhodo-dendron death and have wiped out whole collections and thousands of plants of nursery stock. In climates with regular 90°F (32°C) heat in summer, many varieties will be so susceptible to these diseases that they are not worth attempting, and considerable effort in soil and soil temperature moderation is required.

Root Rot/Wilt (*Phytophthora*)
Phytophthora cinnamoni is a root disease that is usually fatal and often kills a plant extremely quickly. The symptoms are (usually) a sudden collapse during the growing season of the

whole plant or several plants in one area of the garden. Check the roots and cut into the stem of the plant. The disease is characterized by the roots turning a deep brown color (rather than white as healthy growing roots should be). If you scrape away the bark at ground level, you will find the cambium layer below the bark has been stained a dark reddish-brown.

The disease is caused by inadequate drainage and high soil temperatures. The combination of these is very often fatal to rhododendrons. It is most common in areas with hot summers but can occur anywhere if poor drainage in allowed to occur. Plants in containers are particularly susceptible (see page 34).

To avoid the disease, ensure that the planting area is well prepared with coarse organic matter which will allow improved drainage and aeration. Freshly composted bark has been shown to have some root-rot resistant properties and is the most popular medium for container growing in North America. Ensure that the soil where the rhododendrons are growing is not allowed to become compacted by people or animals walking over it. In warmer climates, growing in shade and mulching (see page 43) will help to keep the soil temperature down. In Germany, most varieties of rhododendron are grafted as this seems to increase the tolerance to poorly drained soils. In areas with heavy clay soils, the best practice is often to plant above soil level, either in raised beds or by mounding up the soil around the root of the plant.

Susceptible varieties: Most members of subsections Taliensia (e.g., *R. phaeochrysum*), subsection Neriiflora (e.g., *R. dichroanthum*), and many other species such as *R. souliei* and *R. lanatum*. Most larger yellow hybrids (which are almost all derived from *R. wardii*), such as "Hotei" and "Goldkrone," are also susceptible, as are many of the smaller leaved or alpine species and hybrids. Most larger-growing hybrids (other than in yellow shades) and most azaleas are more heat tolerant and less susceptible. One or two cultivars such as "Roseum Elegans" and "Cadis" are known to be particularly resistant to *Phytophthora*.

If you remove a plant that has died of this disease, dispose of the whole plant including all of the rootball. There is little point in replacing it with the same or a similar variety without doing something to improve the drainage or decrease the soil temperature. It is also prudent to remove the soil that surrounded the dead plant's rootball, as it will have many fungal spores in it. There are several chemicals on the market, mostly not available to amateurs, that can be used as a drench to suppress *Phytophthora*. Good hygiene and optimum planting conditions should be used as none of these fungicides will eradicate the fungus, just control it temporarily.

Stem Dieback (*Botryosphaeria*, *Phytophthora cactorum* and Other Species)

These are serious diseases of rhododendrons in regions with considerable summer heat such as eastern North America. Both are characterized by the sudden wilting and death of a branch or part of a plant, and they tend to attack where plants have been physically damaged in some way (including pruning).

With both diseases, the inside of the wilted stem will have turned brown. The dead stem must be cut out well into green wood in the healthy part of the plant and the dead branch should be removed or burnt (not composted). Ensure that shears are sterilized using bleach or alcohol, to avoid spreading the disease. Good hygiene, adequate air circulation and moderate use of fertilizer all help prevent the diseases. *Botryosphaeria* can begin as leaf spot and soon causes stem dieback.

Honey Fungus (*Armillaria*)

There are many species of honey fungus or *Armillaria* that occur in different parts of the world, most of which feed exclusively on decaying matter. Several species unfortunately are also able to colonize and weaken or kill living plants, and rhododendrons are particularly susceptible.

Sometimes sending up conspicuous fruiting bodies, the main part of the fungus lives underground, sending out vigorous rhizomorphs (commonly known as bootlaces) which colonize both dead and living tree and plant roots. Apparently the world's largest living thing is a species of honey fungus in North America!

Almost exclusively, gardens with a honey fungus problem are those with lots of old tree-stumps in the ground. Of course, one can glibly recommend that all tree roots are removed, but when the extent of the root system of a mature broad leaf such as elm, beech, or sycamore is appreciated, it becomes apparent that this is often impossible.

In our own garden at Glendoick, the remains of massive old elms killed by Dutch Elm disease are the source of much of our infection. Other parts of the world where I have seen considerable problems are in southwestern England, Sweden, and California.

Digging out a dead plant killed by honey fungus will usually reveal the tell-tale black bootlaces that have run through the rootball and into the stem, virtually strangling it in severe cases. Symptoms vary from yellowing of leaves, poor leaf retention, poor growth length, partial dieback of branches on the plant, or sudden total collapse. Often a "last gasp" attempt to flower heavily will be made. There is little doubt that stressed plants (by waterlogging, drought, etc.) are more susceptible to the fungus. Certain species such as *R. lacteum*, most of subsection Taliensia and many in subsection Neriiflora are particularly at risk, while many hybrids seem to be able to withstand having the fungus engulfing their roots, though it usually reduces their vigor.

To prevent the fungus occurring, it is advisable to remove the roots of trees wherever possible. Apart from this, there is very little you can do, other than using barriers to keep it from spreading. The fungus usually remains close to the surface, seldom deeper than 12–18 in. (30–45cm) in lighter soils, though it is said to go deeper in clay soils, so heavy-duty plastic and other materials can be used to make impermeable barriers rather like underground walls. Alternatively, plants can have an underground wall made in a circle around the rootball.

Raised beds with a solid lining are another solution, but ensure there is adequate drainage: try to construct them on a slope if possible. We have tried using permeable membranes, but the fungus appears to be able to penetrate these. There are various phenolic compounds that may help to control honey fungus. These are expensive and they can only be safely used around mature plants. The fungus will usually return if there is infection nearby.

Petal Blight (*Ovulinia*)

This fungal disease is one of the most upsetting as it ruins the flowers you have waited so long to enjoy. Long associated with warmer parts of the rhododendron growing world such as the southeastern United States, it has begun to be a problem in much of North America, parts of Europe, and Australasia.

Infected flowers first exhibit small spots that appear water-soaked. These rapidly enlarge, turning the petals into a slimy gray mass that sinks limply onto the leaves below. It can even strike before the flowers open.

It takes 2–3 days for the flowers to be completely ruined and a whole bush or group of plants can quickly be affected. The destroyed petals, when dry, stick to the foliage and create white patches that turn to black fruiting bodies that will infect the following year's flowers. The disease usually occurs during moist weather at flowering time, especially if accompanied by warmth and poor air circulation. Watering overhead so that it wets the flowers is to be avoided, if possible.

The disease is particularly devastating on plants in greenhouses and cold frames, and it seems to cause the most widespread damage on evergreen azaleas. If you acquire an infected plant, it is well worth removing and destroying all blooms immediately so that the spores cannot be spread. If you have a large amount of infection, it may be necessary to spray with a fungicide when buds start to show color and at weekly intervals until the flowers drop. Keeping the foliage, and especially the flowers, as dry as possible is the best way to avoid the disease. *Botrytis* causes similar, less devastating symptoms, especially on indoor plants that are watered overhead. It differs from petal blight in the lack of black fruiting bodies.

Leaf Gall

This bacterial disease is found on wild populations of some species and is also found in gardens on some species, hybrids, and especially on evergreen/ Japanese azaleas and *R. ferrugineum* and its hybrids. It is an unsightly disease characterized by green, pink, or red swellings on the leaves, shoots, or occasionally flowers. They should be picked off and destroyed and the problem often arises only once a season.

Leaf galls on *R. ferrugineum*. This problem is very commonly observed on evergreen azalea varieties. Picking the galls off is the most common solution

Weather-related and Physical Problems

Sunburn

Rhododendron and azalea varieties vary greatly in their ability to withstand hot sun. In Scotland, sunburn is rarely a problem, while in the south of England a hot summer can cause considerable foliage damage. In southeastern North America and California, most rhododendrons need shade to avoid sunburn.

The key here is to use the minimum shade required to protect the foliage. Too much shade means drawn and leggy plants that seldom flower. The problem with shade is that as your trees grow, the shade increases. Mild sunburn turns leaves bright yellow, while a more severe attack will burn the leaves to a crisp. Once it has happened, there is not much you can do to avoid the problem apart from providing extra shade.. There are many varieties known for their sun-tolerant qualities, such as "Gomer Waterer," "Purple Gem," and "Jean Marie de Montague."

Above: Sunburnt new growth is characterized by yellowing of the leaves and burnt patches. This variety requires more shade.

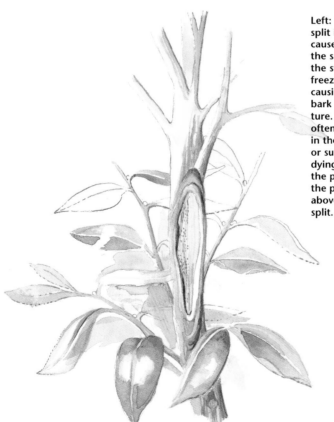

Left: Bark split is caused by the sap in the stem freezing and causing the bark to rupture. This often results in the slow or sudden dying back of the part of the plant above the split.

Spring Frost

Spring frosts are undoubtedly the single most frustrating thing that rhododendron growers have to put up with in many areas. Few rhododendrons have frost-resistant flowers or growth and all too often those long-admired buds are open or are just about to open when a few degrees of frost turns everything brown. This problem is perhaps most extreme in the maritime climate of the British Isles, where mild winters can bring plants into flower as early as late winter and early spring and then see the return of frost in mid- or late spring.

Early varieties are always going to be vulnerable to damage, especially if you garden inland or in a frost pocket. Because frost flows downward, hollows such as river beds will be particularly vulnerable. Surrounding higher ground may escape the worst effects, so locate plants with care. Overhead shade from trees will also moderate the temperature a degree or two, which can often make the difference between damage and escaping virtually unscathed. A few early-flowering varieties such as *R. lapponicum* and *R. hippophaeoides* have frost-resistant flowers, while one or two others including the very popular "Ptarmigan" and "Christmas Cheer" open flowers in batches over a long period so if one flush is frosted, another one soon opens.

You can, of course, put artificial protection over early flowering plants. The problem is that the best protection is afforded by covering but not touching the plants and this is often hard to achieve. Use textiles rather than sheet

71

polyethylene or plastic if possible: old sacks and bed sheets, bubble plastic, or spun polypropylene (sold specifically for this purpose) are all effective. Try to keep the material dry as the weight of damp cloth is often a problem, and wet material is less effective in keeping frost off. Covers are often blown away and one can expend much energy trying to attach covers that will stay put. A rather drastic method that does work is to leave sprinklers on your plants during frosty nights.

Having the flowers frosted does no long-term damage to the plant. Even when growth is badly damaged and looks distorted and unsightly, the plant will usually recover well and put on new growth or it can be pruned off and will be replaced from lateral buds.

Long-term damage can be caused by bark split when sap running in the stem is frozen, busting the outer layer of bark. Often the plant looks healthy for a few months and then the split branch will die off. In the case of young plants, they can easily be killed outright. Species such as *R. yunnanense* and certain forms of *R. augustinii* are particularly vulnerable as small plants. They usually get tougher and more resistant with age. Sometimes the wound will heal over time, but if not, you may have to prune back to below where the split occurred. Bark split is

usually caused by spring frosts but can also occur in autumn in late-growing varieties such as those with *R. griersonianum* and *R. auriculatum* parentage. ("Vanessa Pastel" and "Polar Bear," for instance).

Wind Damage

Leaves broken at the petiole and ragged or brown-edged leaves are a sure sign of wind damage. See page 19 for a discussion of shelter.

Cold

As well as spring frosts, midwinter cold can be very damaging. This is usually seen in browned, brittle foliage, not to mention brown and dead flower buds. Even the hardiest varieties can be severely damaged by a combination of frozen ground with sun and/or wind. This causes foliage desiccation and can defoliate a plant. Prudent use of shade and shelter is the way to alleviate this (see page 16).

Everyone likes to grow plants of borderline hardiness, making use of the most favorable, sheltered sites in the garden. If a variety is on the tender

Below: Frost damage on the flowers of *R. wardii* after a mild frost. In a harder frost, the flowers would have been completely spoiled.

side for your area, then extreme winters will cause substantial problems or even death. In colder parts of continental Europe and many of the eastern regions of the U.S.A. and Canada, the majority of rhododendron hybrids, and especially species, simply are not hardy enough to survive the winter temperatures, so the choice of which varieties to grow is crucial.

The ironclads are an increasingly large group bred to withstand -25°F (-32°C). The early crosses in this group were made in Europe, especially by Waterers in England, but there are many hybridizers, such as American David Leach, who have greatly increased the range.

Right: Late frosts have damaged the already emerging new growth of *R. wiltonii*. If such damage is severe, it is often best to prune it off, encouraging new growth to come from below.

Yellow Leaves

Yellow leaves are simply a sign that the plant is not happy, and this can be caused by many different factors (or a combination of them). If the whole leaf is yellow, the cause is usually sunburn or starvation. If yellowing is more pronounced on the blade of the leaf, with greener veins (chlorosis), the cause is more likely to be mineral (too much or too little) or pH related. The following can cause yellow leaves:

- Poor drainage from heavy or compacted soil.
- Drought through lack of rain or watering, or competition from tree roots.
- Planting too deeply. The top of the rootball should be just below the surface of the soil.
- Nitrogen deficiency. The plant is starving. This can be easily remedied through feeding.
- pH is too high (or occasionally too low). Test your soil pH.
- Mineral deficiency. This is fairly rare and it requires a soil analysis to prove. If you have ruled out the other possibilities in the above list, it may be worth applying trace elements, which are available on their own or in combination with fertilizers. Sequestered or chelated iron is often recommended as a catch-all cure for yellow leaves. Unless you have an iron deficiency, this is an expensive remedy that may do little more than provide a little fertilizer.

Lichen

This often forms on old, straggly specimens, particularly when they have few leaves and are lacking in vigor. Evergreen azaleas and deciduous azaleas seem particularly prone. You can scrub lichen off, but it is a sign of poor soil conditions, lack of fertilizer, or old age. It can best be dealt with by rejuvenating the plants through pruning and fertilizing or by throwing them out and starting again. Lichen grows on weak plants rather than causing the weakness.

No Flowers—Buds Do Not Open

This is most likely to be caused by frost, either in mid-winter by the hardest frosts of the year, or in spring when the buds are swelling and about to open. Certain varieties such as *R. pemakoense* have very frost-vulnerable swelling buds, while many species in subsection Maddenia have buds which are easily destroyed even by quite mild winter frosts. A variety which always has its buds frosted, unless it has fine foliage, may not be worth space in your garden. If the dead buds are covered with spore-laden black bristles, you have bud blast, a disease that affects a few species and hybrids such as *R. maximum* and "Cunningham's White." It is usually not serious enough to warrant spraying, but you can use a suitable fungicide if necessary.

No Flowers—No Flower Buds

There are several possibilities why rhododendrons may not flower freely:

- Too much shade. This is very common in North America where, in order to regulate sun and soil temperature, plants are placed in deep shade. This allows healthy, if straggly growth, but can inhibit flowering. The more light you can give a plant, the more likely it is to flower, so there is a trade-off between the need for shade and the need for light.

- The variety takes many years to flower. Some hybrids and many species need to be quite old before they start flowering. This particularly applies to the large-leaved species such as *R. sinogrande* and some of the species in subsection Taliensia. Some species such as the infamous *R. pronum* hardly ever flower in cultivation. Thankfully, this species is mainly grown for its foliage! Many species do not flower well every year and, especially after a heavy flowering year, they will take a rest.

- Kindness. Rhododendrons flower in order to reproduce. A contented, well-fed, well-watered, well-shaded plant may not feel any need to reproduce, as it perceives no threat to its survival. Do not feed after mid-summer, as this encourages growth at the expense of flowers. Nurserymen cut down watering in late summer to stress plants into flowering the following year. If all else, including threats fail, then try a bit of root pruning. You can even lift a plant and replace it in its hole.

Buying and Collecting

Obtaining the Best Plants

Rhododendrons are one of the more tricky genera to grow well commercially and, due to the sheer number of varieties available, it may take some searching to find what you are looking for. If you want to buy species and more unusual hybrids, you will have to go to one of the many specialist nurseries, some of which offer between 500-1,000 different varieties or more. Many have a mail order service.

Traditionally, rhododendrons have been purchased bare-rooted from nurseries when dormant in autumn, winter, and early spring to be planted before the onset of new growth in the spring. Buying from specialty nurseries is usually cheaper than buying from garden centers

and, most importantly, you are more likely to get correctly named stock.

Rhododendrons are hard to identify, partly because there are so many of them, and the naming of species is particularly poor. Species should be grown from hand-pollinated seed, wild-collected seed (preferably with a collector's number), cuttings, or grafts. Never accept plants that have been dug up from the wild; they will almost certainly fail, and it is totally unethical.

These days, most rhododendrons are probably bought from garden centers and are container-grown; the largest range is usually held in spring, as it is the flowering season. While there is no reason why a well looked-after, container-grown rhododendron should not thrive once planted in the garden, it pays to know what to avoid. Modern nursery practice involves forcing container plants as fast as possible to a salable size using fertilizer, heat, and artificial protection to ensure good budding and healthy foliage. This treatment can result in a plant that takes a considerable time to recover when planted in the garden. This is especially true if a plant is becoming root-bound in its pot. Rhododendron roots are shallow and

spreading, while the pots they grow in are narrow and deep.

I have often seen pot-bound rhododendrons planted in gardens where, several years later, the pot shape is still visible when roots are inspected. Very little in the way of new roots have been put out into the surrounding soil, resulting in a corresponding lack of healthy new growth and flower buds. Such plants-to-avoid are usually found in garden centers in late summer or early autumn, looking forlorn and lonely, vainly hoping someone will take pity on them. The rootball will invariably have dried out and there may be roots coming out the drainage holes. Look out for signs of powdery mildew (see page 66). Do not buy such plants.

Left: Evergreen azaleas associated with heathers and conifers at Rosemoor Garden, Devon.

Opposite: A fine display of azaleas sold as houseplants at a garden center. The tall azalea is grown as a half standard.

Grafted Plants

For some people, grafted plants have a bad reputation. This is largely due to the use of *R. ponticum* as an understock. This species is so vigorous that it constantly sends up suckers which, if not removed, gradually take all the sap from the plant, eventually causing the grafted variety to die off. This is incorrectly referred to as "reverting." Few nurseries graft onto *R. ponticum* these days, but it is always worth enquiring what the rootstock was. If you do not get an answer, do not buy. Most now use "Cunningham's White," "County of York," and other rootstocks that throw far fewer suckers.

Do not buy grafts less than two years old as it takes this long to know whether the graft has taken or not. Avoid plants with an unnatural bulge where the union is, as this indicates incompatibility: in the long term, these usually fail. In Germany and Holland, almost all larger hybrids are grafted. This makes them expensive, but it does allow tolerance of poorer growing conditions.

Right: "Crest" is one of the finest yellow hybrids. Several years ago many plants produced by tissue culture turned out to have smaller-than-normal leaves and small, poor flowers. Thankfully, this problem has been rectified.

Left: When buying a grafted plant, try to ensure that a strong union has been formed between rootstock and the variety grafted on top, and that there is no exaggerated bulge at the union.

Tissue Culture

Most larger hybrids these days are produced by tissue-culture. As long as correct procedures have been followed, there is nothing wrong with this technique, but unfortunately, things can go wrong. Avoid unnaturally bushy plants with thin stems and smaller-than-normal leaves. These plants are in suspended juvenility, which they never grow out of, caused by high rates of hormones. There were thousands of "Crest" like this sold several years ago.

Collecting Rhododendrons

There are many rhododendron societies worldwide, from North America to Europe, Japan, Australia, New Zealand, and elsewhere. These reflect the serious addiction to collecting rhododendrons many people have.

Most people start growing some of the widely available, readily grown hybrids and gradually start to notice the qualities of other choice varieties when they visit some of the great collections. As people's knowledge and enthusiasm increases, they tend to get more and more hooked on species. There are several reasons for this; the most obvious is that they often have more interesting foliage. There is admittedly also a degree of snobbery involved.

One of the most interesting facets of species collecting is the collector's number. Most of the great early collectors, as well as many contemporary ones, collect seed in the wild under a collector's number. This means that the collector assigns a number to the seed packet and keeps notes on when and where the plant was collected, how large it was, and what grew with it. Often a specimen of the plant is pressed and sent back to a botanic garden.

For example: *R. macabeanum* KW 7724 was collected by Frank Kingdon Ward on his 1927-28 expedition to India, Tibet, and Burma. In his field notes, he records it as: "a forest tree with handsome foliage, truss with 12–18 flowers … it goes right to the summit where it forms forests … it should be hardy." He records the location as Mt. Javpo, Naga Hills, Assam, occurring from 8–10,000 ft. (2.5–3,000m), and he collected the seed on December 1, 1927. The seed from this collection was distributed far and wide, but wherever the plants have ended up, as long the collection number was retained, the plant's origin can be traced. It turns out that KW 7724 was the first introduction of the species *R. macabeanum*, discovered by Sir George Watt 40 years earlier.

Above: *R. macabeanum* is one of the finest of the large-leaved species with spectacular yellow flowers and handsome foliage. It requires wind shelter and a favorable climate.

Rhododendron species are quite widely available with a collector's number, either propagated from selected clones in collections, or as seedlings grown from recent expeditions to the wild. The latter are perhaps the most exciting, as each seedling is unique and you may be lucky enough to have one of the best. If you buy species with a collector's number, or grow them from seed, keep the collector's number on the label, so that the plant always carries its own coded identity card. The number can later be decoded, with a bit of research, allowing each plant to tell its own story. This makes a collection more interesting, more complete, and more fun. It is very exciting as a collector to find plants with your numbers on them growing well in far-flung corners of the globe.

Plant
Directory

There are about 900 species of rhododendrons and azaleas and around 15,000 named hybrids so, in a book this size, it is only possible to survey a small percentage of what is available. Many new hybrids are named every year. A few of them become successful and perhaps one a year joins the list as a nurseryman's standard.

There are specialist nurseries all over the rhododendron-growing world that offer several hundred varieties; many provide a mail order service. I have tried to cover a selection of the best of the widely available varieties for all of the diverse climates of the rhododendron-growing world. Some of the most promising of the newer varieties are also included.

Contents

Hardiness

Hardiness is difficult to quantify precisely, as it depends on the timing of the cold weather. Many plants that are mid-winter-hardy are more vulnerable to damage in early autumn or late spring. The combination of high summer temperatures and cold winters cannot be tolerated by many varieties. The ratings here are an extension and adaptation of those used by the Royal Horticultural Society for rhododendrons.

H0 32°F (0°C) minimum. USDA 10-(9b) +/- frost free
Greenhouse culture, except in mildest areas such as parts of California, Hawaii, Australia, and north New Zealand.

H1 15°F to 20°F (-10°C to -8°C) USDA 8b-9a
Greenhouse culture, except for milder areas such as those above and also mildest western U.K. gardens.

H2 10°F (-12°C) minimum USDA 8a
Hardy outdoors in milder parts of U.K. (such as Cornwall, Argyll), southern Ireland, most of California, also west Vancouver Island, Canada, most of New Zealand, Tasmania.

H3 5°F (-15°C) minimum USDA 7b
Hardy in a sheltered site in most U.K., Coastal France and northern Italy and Pacific Northwest gardens, but may be damaged in severest winters. Often early into flower and growth.

H4 0°F (-18°C) minimum USDA 7a
Hardy in all but coldest parts of Pacific Northwest and U.K., France and northern Italy, around Bergen (Norway) and mildest parts of northeastern U.S.A. such as Cape Cod and parts of Long Island.

H5 -10°F (-23°C) minimum USDA 6
Hardy anywhere in the U.K. and moderate parts of Europe such as Holland, southern Sweden, coastal Denmark, favorable parts of Germany, etc, moderate parts of northeastern U.S.A. and eastern Canada.

H6 -20°F (-29°C) minimum USDA 5
Hardy in colder parts of Germany and Scandinavia, New York, Nova Scotia, etc.

H7 Colder than -20°F (-29°C) USDA 4b(-a)
Ironclads. These are the hardiest varieties suitable for the coldest areas suitable for growing rhododendrons, including parts of eastern Europe and much of inland eastern U.S.A. and Canada. Most are heat tolerant.

Height

Heights given are those attainable as a plant after 10–15 years. Most will eventually grow much bigger under ideal conditions, and reach a considerable age. Plants in dry and cold climates grow more slowly than those in mild and wet climates that have long growing seasons.

Dwarf To 16 in. (40cm) usually spreading, wider than high.

Semi-dwarf 16 in.–2½ ft. (40–80cm), often spreading wider than high.

Low 2½–4½ ft. (80–135cm), sometimes spreading wider than high.

Medium 4½ ft–6 ft. (35–190cm), considerably more with time.

Tall 6 ft. (190cm) and more; much larger over time.

FLOWERING TIME

In mild and maritime
climates, the flowering
season can cover seven
months or more, while in
severe climates, the flowering season is compressed
into a three-month period.
We find with the vagaries
of the British climate,
there is considerable
variation from year to
year, especially with early
flowering varieties.

*R. degroni-
anum* is a
very tough
Japanese
species, with
the hardiest
forms suitable
for severe
climates.

Dwarf and Low-Growing Varieties

This section includes varieties most suitable for the smaller garden. Although many of them can tolerate cold winters, most small-leaved alpine types are not suitable for areas with hot summers. This group includes the very popular "yak" hybrids bred from the species *R. yakushimanum*. These are useful for their full, rounded trusses, their relatively late-flowering, their fine foliage, and compact habit. Many are very hardy and their only drawback is that a large number of them have flowers that fade. Most of the varieties listed are widely available from garden centers.

"Arctic Tern" is a most unusual low-growing hybrid with masses of tiny white flowers in late May.

"April" Hybrids
H7 Low *E-M*

This is a range of double-flowered, very hardy hybrids bred for severe northern climates. The flowers are very showy but the plants tend to be semi-deciduous and need pruning, and some are susceptible to root rot. "April Snow," "April Gem," and "April White" have double white flowers. "April Mist" and "April Rose," "Weston's Pink Diamond," and "Staccato" have double pink flowers. There are several others.

"Arctic Tern"
H4-5 Low *ML-L*

A useful late-flowered, small-leaved dwarf. Rounded trusses of a mass of tiny white flowers. Its habit its rather rangy, requiring pruning, and it is susceptible to rust.

"Blue Diamond"
H4-5 Low *EM-M*

Masses of bluish-purple flowers. Small leaves. Tends to suffer from leaf spot. "Blue Tit" is very similar, with paler flowers and a similar tendency to leaf spot. Many similar hybrids have been raised, many of which have better foliage.

"Bow Bells"
H4-5 Low *EM-M*

Light pink, bell-shaped flowers in loose trusses on a tidy plant with oval leaves and bronzy new growth. Very popular in areas of moderate climate.

calostrotum
H4-5 Dwarf-Low *EM-L*

This is a variable small-leaved species. Ssp. calostrotum has purple or pink flowers. "Gigha" is a bright pink, large-flowered selection with gray-blue foliage. Can be hard to please. Ssp. *keleticum* has pointed leaves, a dense habit, and flat-faced purple flowers, relatively late for a dwarf. The slowest-growing and most compact forms are known as Radicans Group.

"Caroline Albrook"
H5 Low *M-ML*

Frilly lavender-pink flowers in full trusses which fade to pale lavender. A tough, compact "yak" hybrid that is free-flowering. "Hoppy" is taller growing and "Centennial Celebration" is a popular American hybrid of similar color.

campylogynum
H4 Dwarf/Semi-dwarf *M*

One of the most captivating of the dwarf species, with its little thimbles of red, purple, pink or white flowers held above the foliage on long stalks. Best in moderate climates with cool summers. One of the best cultivars ever produced. It is easy to grow as a bush or standard and, although the stems are rather short, it can be grown in a hanging basket.

"Carmen"
H4 Dwarf *EM-M*

Deep red, waxy flowers on a neat grower, which likes cool roots in summer.

"Cilipense"
H3-4 Semi-dwarf *E*

Pink buds open to pale pink flowers which fade to white. Small leaves on a fairly compact and tidy plant. Magnificent at its best, but its buds and flowers are so prone to frost damage, it is only worth growing in mild areas. "Snow Lady" and "Lucy Lou" are equally early flowering with pure white flowers and hairy, oval leaves. "Lucy Lou" has the more compact habit.

"Curlew"
H4 Dwarf *EM-M*

The best-known of the Glendoick "bird" hybrids. A compact spreader with relatively large yellow flowers, spotted red. Flowers vulnerable to frost damage. Dislikes hot summers. "Chikor" has smaller leaves and flowers, "Princess Anne" and "Shamrock" have smaller and paler flowers.

dendrocharis
H4-5 Dwarf *E-EM*

One of the most exciting new species introductions of recent years. Small deep green, hairy leaves on a neat, compact plant. Relatively large deep pink flowers. Needs good drainage.

"Egret," raised by the author's father, is a fine, compact dwarf hybrid with masses of tiny, white bell-shaped flowers.

"Dopey"
H4 Low *ML*

One of the "seven dwarf" series of "yak" hybrids, this has among the best, unfading, red flowers of this group. Pale green foliage, somewhat subject to mildew. "Titian Beauty" is slower growing with small flowers, of an equally good red, and more handsome foliage with indumentum on the leaf lower surface. "Skookum" (H6) is a much hardier alternative for severe climates. Fairly compact, with full rounded trusses of strong red.

"Dora Amateis"
H5-6 Semi-dwarf *EM-M*

One of the best dwarf hybrids for colder areas. Masses of pure white flowers with green markings. A rather spreading habit. Sometimes has yellowish foliage.

"Egret"
H4 Dwarf/Semi-dwarf *M*

Masses of tiny white bells on a compact plant with very small deep green leaves. Very distinctive.

"Elisabeth Hobbie"
H5 Low *EM-M*

One of the best selling low-growing red hybrids. Very easy to please and reliable. Loose trusses of bright red flowers on a dense and compact grower. There are many very similar hybrids such as "Scarlet Wonder," "Baden Baden" (which has a twist in the leaf), and "Bengal."

"Elizabeth Lockhart"
H4 Low *EM-M*

Mainly grown for its deep reddish-purple leaves. Flowers deep red. Oval leaves on a compact bush. Needs to be grown in shade to retain leaf color. "Elizabeth Red Foliage" (H4) has red flowers and bronzy-red new growth which remains this color for several months.

The "yak" hybrid "Fantastica" has become one of the most popular of the many hybrids of the species *R. yakushimanum*. The inside of the corolla fades quicker than the outside, giving a very attractive, two-toned effect.

"Fantastica"
H5-6 Low *M-ML*

One of the most spectacular "yak" hybrids. Full, rounded trusses open bright pink and fade to off-white. The rim of each flower remains deeper than the center, giving a most attractive effect. There are many other pink "yak" hybrids of similar coloring: some of the most popular include "Morgenrot" (H5) Reddish flowers, fading to deep pink, and "Surrey Heath" (H4) with a very dense habit and pink flowers.

fastigiatum
H5-6 Dwarf *EM-M*

This popular, compact and dwarf species has masses of small purplish-blue flowers and tiny bluish-green leaves. Very good in cooler areas and very hardy, but this species and its relatives dislike hot summers. *R. impeditum* is very similar species and most of what is sold under this name is in fact *R. fastigiatum*. *R. russatum* is taller growing with very deep purple flowers in the best forms.

ferrugineum
H5-6 Semi-dwarf-Low *L-VL*

The "Alpenrose" is a useful late-flowering species with small pink flowers on a small-leaved, compact grower. Very hardy but needs good drainage. Its close relative, *R. hirsutum*, will tolerate near neutral soil.

forrestii
H4 Dwarf *E-EM*

Fine, waxy-red flowers on a mounding or prostrate plant with small oval leaves. Needs cool conditions for both foliage and roots.

"Gartendirektor Rieger"
H5 Low-Medium *M*

A fine, vigorous and easy hybrid with large cream flowers, spotted red in an open-topped truss. Leaves are deep-green and somewhat rounded. Less hardy and smaller leaved hybrids with creamy, bell-shaped flowers include "Moonstone" and "Cowslip."

R. haematodes is a very low-growing species with waxy red flowers and small dark green leaves with thick indumentum on the lower surface.

"Ginny Gee"
H5-6 Dwarf *EM*

This award-winning hybrid is one of the most popular dwarf hybrids. Masses of pale pink and white flowers virtually hide the foliage. Easy and vigorous but compact. Two newly introduced similar hybrids are "Crane" (raised by the author) and "June Bee." Both have masses of creamy-white flowers.

"Golden Torch"
H4 Low *ML*

The name is a misnomer as this is a cream-colored "yak" hybrid, severely overrated in my opinion, but popular in moderate areas. Foliage tends to be yellowish. Needs good drainage.

"Grumpy"
H4 Low *EM-M*

Cream-colored flowers, with pink flushing in flat-topped trusses on a fairly tidy "yak" hybrid with dark green leaves and indumentum on the lower surface. Very similar are its sister seedlings "Dusty Miller" with pale pink flowers and the cream and apricot "Molly Miller." All these have insipid flowers, but some find them attractive.

haematodes
H4-5 Low *M-L*

This is a fine compact foliage plant with deep green leaves and thick woolly indumentum on the underside. The very fine red flowers may take a few years to appear. Needs good drainage.

"Hummingbird"
H3-4 Low *EM-M*

There are several clones of this hybrid in commerce. Cherry to rose red bells hang down over the foliage on long stalks. Fine foliage on a dense, compact grower.

hypoleuceum (formerly *Ledum*)
H5 Semi-dwarf *M-ML*

The ledums have recently been reclassified as part of the genus *Rhododendron*. All have rounded trusses of a mass of tiny white flowers. They have aromatic leaves which tend to curl up, turn brown and look dead in winter. Species include *R. groenlandicum* and *R. neoglandulosum* from North America, and *R. tomentosum* and *R. hypoleucum* from Europe and Asia.

keiskei
H5-6 Dwarf/Semi-dwarf *EM-M*

One of the hardiest dwarf species. Pale yellow flowers, usually spotted red. The most dwarf form, usually grown as "Yaku Fairy" is one of the slowest-growing of all dwarfs with a near prostrate habit and fine pale yellow flowers.

"Ken Janeck"
H6 Low *M*

One of the finest "yak" hybrids for foliage, with the underside of the leaf and the upper surface on the young growth covered with indumentum. Compact and dense growing with fine pale pink flowers which fade to white. "Mist Maiden" is very similar. "Crete" (H6-7) is hardier but has less impressive flowers. "Yaku Princess" (H5-6) is taller growing with similar flowers.

lepidostylum
H4-5 Semi-dwarf *L*

This species is mainly grown for its very showy, glaucous-blue young growth on a spreading plant. The small, yellow flowers tend to be hidden in the foliage.

R. hypoleucum (*Ledum hypoleucum*) with its tiny white flowers and aromatic foliage. Until recently, considered a separate genus, the Ledums have recently been classified within the genus *Rhododendron*.

"Linda"
H5-6 Low *M*

One of the many hybrids of *R. williamsianum* (see below). Egg-shaped, pale green leaves and frilly, bright pink flowers in showy trusses. Good habit and one of the latest of this group in flower and growth. Other similar hybrids include "Osmar" (H5) and "Oudijk's Sensation" (H5). All these have pendulous bell-shaped pink flowers and bronzy young leaves.

"Mary Fleming"
H6 Semi-dwarf-Low *E-EM*

This is one of the best hybrids of this type for Eastern North America as it is sun and heat tolerant as well as very tough. Clusters of yellowish-cream flowers, shaded pink.

minus
H3-7 Low *EM-ML*

This East Coast native is one of the hardiest lepidote (scaly-leaved) rhododendrons and has been much used as a parent. Pink flowers (occasionally white) on a fairly tidy bush. Carolinianum

Group includes hardiest (H7) forms while var. *chapmanii* (H3) is not cold-hardy but, as it comes from Florida, is very heat tolerant.

"Patty Bee"
H5 Dwarf EM

One of the most popular of the dwarf yellow hybrids and one of the hardier ones. Masses of pale yellow flowers on a very compact plant. A winner of several awards.

"Penheale Blue"
H4-5 Low EM

One of the finest of the low-growing, small-leaved purple-blue hybrids. Fine, deep blue-purple flowers on a fairly compact plant with deep green, healthy foliage. Other similar varieties include "Gristede," "Night Sky," and "Gletschernacht" ("Starry Night").

"Percy Wiseman"
H5 Low ML-L

One of the most popular "yak" hybrids, this extremely free-flowering plant has peachy-pink to cream flowers and rather pale green leaves. Proving to be hardier than first thought.

P.J.M. Group
H7 Low E-EM

P.J.M. in its various forms is probably the world's best-selling hybrid. Rosy-purple flowers on a fairly compact plant with mahogany-purple foliage in winter. The commercial standard low-growing hybrid in northeastern U.S.A. and eastern Canada. Not very successful in southeastern U.S.A. as it is subject to root rot there. There are several clones. "P.J. Mezitt" selected in the U.K. is rather shy flowering. Much better are "P.J.M. Regal," "P.J.M. Victor," and "P.J.M. Elite." These vary slightly in their flowering time and vigor. "Checkmate" is a fine dwarf clone, very free-flowering.

"Linda" is one of the finest of the many R. williamsianum hybrids, most of which have bell-shaped pink flowers and bronzy-colored young leaves.

"Praecox"
H4-5 Low-Medium E

One of the first dwarf hybrids ever raised, but still popular in moderate climates. Masses of pinkish-purple flowers in early spring. We find it best hard pruned every few years to keep the habit dense. "Tessa Rosa" with fine pink flowers and "Tessa Bianca" with white flowers are equally early and very fine.

primuliflorum "Doker LA"
H4 Semi-dwarf M

This is a member of the Pogonanthum Section of species characterized by their (unfortunately unscented) daphne-like flowers. Masses of brightest pink flowers on a neat, tiny-leaved plant. Needs excellent drainage and a near neutral soil. The equally fine *R. trichostomum* is later flowering and more tolerant of hot or dry conditions. This group of species and hybrids are seldom successful in areas with hot summers. "Sarled" with cream flowers and the taller "Maricee" with white flowers are perhaps slightly easier to please.

"Ptarmigan"
H4-5 Dwarf E-EM

The "snow grouse," raised by the author's father, is a useful early-flowering hybrid that opens its pure white flowers over a long period, so some flowers avoid frosts. This spreading plant benefits from pruning when young.

racemosum
H3-5 Semi-dwarf/ Low/Medium *E-M*

This species is very variable in flower color, hardiness, and stature. Masses of small flowers from buds that form in the leaf axils vary from deep pink though pale pink to white. Some forms are straggly, needing pruning, while others are compact and dwarf. Tolerant of dry conditions and some forms may be heat tolerant.

"Ramapo"
H7 Semi-dwarf *EM*

This has long been the most satisfactory low purple-blue for very cold climates, and it is one of the few with a degree of sun and heat tolerance. Pale lavender-blue flowers on a fairly compact grower with fine gray-blue foliage. Its sister "Purple Gem" is less hardy but has darker flowers.

roxieanum
H5 Low *EM-M*

Usually sold as the form var. *oreonastes*, this is one of the finest slow-growing species. Narrow, pointed leaves with indumentum on the underside on a compact plant that is reminiscent of a porcupine. Rounded trusses of light pink to white flowers with red spotting. Often takes a while to start flowering but not as long as the closely related *R. proteoides*, which has smaller leaves and a

very fine compact habit. *R. pronum* with a low, dense habit and fine bluish leaves, rarely flowers at all.

"Ruby Hart"
H3-4 Low *M*

A very fine hybrid for moderate climates with dark green leaves, a compact habit, and very dark, black-red flowers.

sanguineum
H4 Semi-dwarf/ Low *E-ML*

A variable, low-growing species with flowers of red, pink, white, yellow or a combination of colors. It needs very good drainage and cool roots in summer and takes several years to flower freely. *R. dichroanthum* (ML-L) enjoys similar conditions and has orange flowers, or a combination of orange with yellow, pink, or red.

Above: *R. roxieanum* var. *oreonastes* **is one of the finest species for foliage effect. It has white flowers with red spotting.**

Above: "Ruby Hart" **has among the darkest red flowers of any rhododendron.**

Opposite: *R. yakushimanum* **with its excellent foliage and compact habit and fine flowers has made it perhaps the most popular rhododendron species.**

"Schneekrone" (syn. "Snow Crown")
H5-6 Low *M-ML*

One of the most popular "yak" hybrids of this shade, pink buds open to white flowers with red spots. A vigorous, tough and free-flowering plant.

"Sneezy"
H5 Low *M-ML*

One of the seven dwarf "yak" hybrids, this is larger-growing and the most vigorous. Full trusses of frilly, bright pink flowers, with red spotting, fade to pale pink. Not one of the best of the "yaks" for

foliage. "Bashful" is very similar. "Mardi Gras" (H4-5) is more compact with pale pink flowers, fading to white. "Hydon Dawn" (H4) has pink flowers with a deeper center and fine silvery young growth. "Solidarity" (H5-6) has large, deep pink flowers in a fine truss, which fade to pale pink and white. One of the most vigorous "yak" hybrids. Highly rated in eastern parts of the U.S.A.

"Schneekrone" (syn. "Snow Crown")

"Wee Bee"
H5 Dwarf *EM*

A terrible name for a fine plant with masses of rose-pink flowers, deeper on the outside, on a very compact grower with small, dark leaves. Everyone's favorite. Its sister "Too Bee" has darker flowers.

williamsianum
H4-5 Semi-dwarf/Low *EM-M*

The parent of many hybrids, this very attractive species is characterized by its pink, bell-shaped flowers and its small, oval leaves, which are reddish-brown in young growth. Hardy, but the young growth is vulnerable to late frosts.

yakushimanum
H7 Semi-dwarf/Low *ML*

This is perhaps the best known species and certainly the most popular parent of all time, producing the "yak" hybrids such as "Dopey" and "Schneekrone" listed above. Pink buds open to rounded trusses of white flowers. A very dense, compact grower having handsome leaves with thick indumentum on the underside and a silvery covering on the new growth. The clone "Koichiro Wada" F.C.C. is one of the best selections. *R. degronianum* (H5-6) with similar foliage is taller growing with pink flowers.

Left: The very variable *R. augustinii* with masses of purple-blue flowers is one of the finest species of this shade. Best in a woodland setting with some shelter.

Right: The poor leaf retention and extremely free flowering probably indicates that this specimen of a fine red-flowered *R. arboreum* is dying.

Larger Species

Although some of these are very tough and easy, the majority require a certain amount of shelter from wind and, in more southerly climates, a fair amount of shade. Many come into growth and flower in early spring, so are best with some frost protection. Species often take a few years to start flowering and, even then, some will not do so every year. Many of the species make up for this with their magnificent foliage, which is attractive year round. Those listed below are hardy enough for cultivation outdoors in the U.K. and Pacific Northwest of North America; some are suitable for colder climates. Less hardy species are covered in the "tender rhododendrons" section. Seldom available from garden centers, larger species are best purchased from specialist nurseries. You are more likely to get them correctly named this way!

adenogynum
H5-6 Low-Medium *E-M*

This species is a member of subsection Taliensia whose members are prized by collectors for their foliage. All take a few years to flower and most need very good drainage and cool summer conditions. Pale pink to white flowers on a compact plant with fine foliage. *R. balfourianum* is similar with fine pink flowers.

arboreum
H2-4 Tall *E-M*

One of the most variable species, which is not surprising as its wild distribution extends from Sri Lanka through the Himalaya to Yunnan in China. This species is the dominant forest rhododendron (and the national flower) in Nepal, though much of the forest has been cut down. Capable of reaching 100 ft. (30m) in the wild, it can get very large in milder areas. Full, tall trusses of flowers vary from red though pink to white. Thick, stiff leaves have silvery or reddish-brown indumentum on the underside. The red forms tend to be the least hardy. *R. niveum* (H4) is a closely related, lower-growing species with distinctive purple flowers.

augustinii
H3-4 Medium *EM-M*

This species is one of the species in subsection Triflora. This subsection is characterized by fairly large-growing but small-leaved plants that are usually very free-flowering from a young age. *R. augustinii* is most commonly grown in its purple-blue flowered forms that can be very spectacular. Variable in hardiness and flower color. The closely related *R. concinnum* is hardier and usually has purple or reddish-purple flowers in cultivated forms.

argyrophyllum
H5 Medium-Tall *E-M*

A very variable species from China with pink to white flowers. Usually grown as ssp. *nankingense* with fine pink flowers. *R. insigne* (L) is lower growing with pink flowers and a leaf underside covered with an metal-like indumentum.

auriculatum
H4-5 Tall VL

The latest of the larger species to flower, this magnificent plant has scented white flowers, which open in late summer in the northern hemisphere. Under good conditions it grows into a huge, vase-shaped specimen. Its only drawback, apart from needing plenty of room, is that it grows very late in the season and is, therefore, vulnerable to early autumn frosts.

barbatum
H3-4 Medium-Tall VE-EM

At its best this is one of the finest red-flowered species for moderate climates. Full, rounded trusses of brightest scarlet flowers on an upright plant with bristles on the leaf stalks and very fine, peeling, purplish bark. Needs some shelter. *R. argipeplum* differs only in the presence of indumentum on the leaf underside. *R. strigillosum*, also with early red flowers, has a more spreading habit and distinctive recurved leaves. The rare *R. exasperatum* has similar red flowers but is mainly grown for its wonderful purple tinged new growth and bristly leaves.

Left: For foliage, few species rival *R. bureauvii* with thick reddish-brown indumentum on the stems and leaf underside, and whitish-fawn new growth

bureavii
H5 Low-Medium EM-M

One of the finest of all species for foliage: Its dark green leaves are quilted beneath with thick reddish-brown indumentum, which also covers the stems. Flowers are usually relatively small, white with reddish spots. The closely related *R. bureaviides* has larger flowers, but the foliage is not quite so striking. *R. elegantulum* is lower-growing and more free-flowering with fine pink flowers and handsome narrow leaves.

calophytum
H5-6 Tall E-EM

The hardiest of the large-leaved species, this massive-growing, handsome plant has long, stiff leaves with large trusses of white flowers, strongly blotched red in the throat. The closely related *R. sutchuenense* (H5) has shorter leaves and pink flowers.

campanulatum
H4 Medium-Tall EM-M

This Himalayan species has variable lavender to white flowers. Foliage is usually handsome with indumentum on the leaf underside. Ssp. *aeruginosum* has fine, glaucous foliage. *R. wallichii* differs in its thinner or absent indumentum.

catawbiense
H7 Low-Medium ML-L

This North American native is one of the hardiest of all species and a parent of many of the hardiest hybrids. It is only worth growing in severest climates. Purplish-pink (occasionally white) flowers on a fairly tidy and compact plant that can take full exposure. *R. maximum* is equally hardy and is useful for its late white or pale pink flowers with a yellow blotch. Tolerant of quite deep shade.

cinnabarinum
H3-4 Medium-Tall EM-L

This very variable species is one of the most distinctive species with its clusters of pendant, tubular flowers in many different colors. All have fairly small leaves and a more or less upright habit and all are subject to powdery mildew disease, though some forms are more susceptible than others. Ssp. *cinnabarinum* usually has orange flowers, "Roylei" Group has red flowers, ssp. *xanthocodon* has yellow flowers and "Concatenans" Group has orange-yellow flowers and glaucous foliage.

dauricum
H6-7 Semi-dwarf-Medium *VE-E*

This very tough deciduous species is a parent of many of the hardiest hybrids such as "P.J.M. Purple", purplish-pink, or white flowers, normally on the bare stems. The small leaves usually develop as the flowers are shed. The clone "Midwinter" flowers in January in the U.K. *R. mucronulatum* (H5-6) is slightly less hardy, usually later flowering and is pink in most commonly cultivated forms. The forms grown as var. *chejuense* are low-growing with fine flowers and good autumn color.

decorum
H3-4 Medium-Tall *M-ML*

This vigorous and easily grown species is useful for moderate climates for its scented pink to white flowers, and its tolerance of relatively dry conditions and near neutral soil. Variable in hardiness and flowering time. The variable R. vernicosum usually has pink or purplish-pink flowers with little or no scent.

Above: One of the hardiest scented species, *R. fortunei* has been an important parent and is a popular plant in severe climates.

Left: The pendulous bells of *R. cinnabarinum* never fail to attract attention. The form shown here is from the Roylei Group. Other forms have orange, yellow or bi-colored flowers.

fortunei
H5-6 Medium-Tall *ML-L*

This is the hardiest scented species and it has been much used in hybridizing. Pale pink or pale lavender flowers fade to white. Smooth, glabrous leaves. Popular in eastern North America.

neriiflorum
H3-4 Low-Tall EM-M

A very variable species, usually grown in its red-flowered forms. Loose trusses of bright red flowers. Leaves usually glabrous.

orbiculare
H4 Low-Medium EM-M

A very distinctive species that has almost round leaves. Deep rose-pink or purplish-pink flowers.

oreodoxa
H5 Medium E-EM

This early flowering species has white, lilac, or pink flowers which are relatively frost-hardy. In most forms they will take a few degrees of frost. This species is most commonly grown as var. *fargesii*, which usually has pink flowers.

pachysanthum
H5 Low EM

First introduced during the 1970s from its native Taiwan, this has become one of the most popular species, due to its outstanding foliage. The leaves are covered with a silvery or fawn indumentum on both upper and lower surfaces which, unlike most species, persists on the upper surface. A dense, compact grower with pale pink or white

flowers. *R. pseudochrysanthum* is closely related, with less indumentum but fine, pale pink to white flowers.

ponticum
H4 Medium ML-L

The infamous wild rhododendron of the British Isles was introduced from eastern Turkey over 200 years ago and has since become a serious invasive weed in areas of high rainfall. It now covers hundreds of acres of western Scotland, Wales, and Cornwall and is very hard to eradicate. In drier parts of the U.K. it stays under control and may be a useful windbreak. Little grown outside the U.K.

rex
H4-5 Tall M-ML

This is the hardiest of the large-leaved species with indumentum and is a very popular garden plant. Huge trusses of pale pink to white flowers with a deep red or purple spotting or blotch in the throat. Deep green, handsome leaves up to 18 in. (45cm) long. Worth attempting even in cold climates. Ssp. *fictolacteum* has slightly smaller leaves. Equally fine. *R. hodgsonii* (H4-5) is usually just as hardy. Fine, large leaves and attractive pinkish bark; flowers pink to magenta.

glischrum
H3-4 Medium-Tall EM-ML

A handsome species with bristly leaves and branches. Flowers pink or purplish-pink with a reddish-purple blotch in the throat, in fine rounded trusses. The related *R. adenosum* (H4) is a little-known species which should be more widely grown. Pink or white flowers on a tidy bush that is quite free-flowering.

hyperythrum
H5-6 Low-Medium EM-M

Usually pure white flowers in rounded trusses on a tidy plant with glabrous leaves that curve down at the edges. Cold and heat tolerant and should be used more as a parent.

lutescens
H3-4 Medium E-EM

This species has smallish, pointed leaves that are reddish or brown in the young growth. Bright yellow flowers in early spring. Rather early into growth, so needs shelter from frosts. The more compact *R. ambiguum* (H5) is hardier and flowers later.

Above: *R. glischrum* is an excellent plant for the woodland garden, with large leaves and showy pinkish-purple flowers with a deeper blotch in the throat.

Right: The infamous *R. ponticum* has naturalized itself in wetter parts of the British Isles where it has become an invasive weed that is very hard to eradicate. Its purple flowers provide a spectacular sight in June.

rubiginosum
H4 Tall *E-EM*

In moderate climates, this is one of the most vigorous species and it is useful as a windbreak or screen. Tolerant of near-neutral soil and fairly dry conditions. Small scaly, leaves and masses of lavender-pink to mauve flowers.

sinogrande
H2-3 Tall *EM-M*

This species has the largest leaves in the genus, reaching a majestic 3 ft. (1m) in length in favorable conditions. Eventually growing enormous, with spectacular trusses of 20 to 50 cream-colored flowers

with a crimson blotch. Takes many years to flower. Requires plenty of shelter. *R. macabeanum* has smaller, more oval leaves and fine yellow flowers.

smirnowii
H5-6 Low-Medium ML-L

A useful, tough species with rounded trusses of pink flowers on a fairly compact plant with indumentum on the leaf lower surface. Some heat and drought resistance.

Above: A white form of *R. souliei*, which has characteristic saucer-shaped flowers. It is often grown in pale and deep pink forms.

Left: *R. yunnanense* is a very common species in its native Yunnan, where it covers huge areas. Very free-flowering in the garden and tolerant of dry conditions, but it is rather vulnerable to bark split as a young plant.

souliei
H4-5 Low-Medium *M*

A beautiful species in its saucer-shaped pink or white flowers. Glabrous and glaucous leaves. Needs excellent drainage and dislikes hot summers, so seldom successful away from cooler northern areas.

thomsonii
H3-4 Medium-Tall EM-M

This fine species has rounded leaves and waxy, red flowers. It is also grown for its beautiful smooth, pinkish bark. Particularly prone to powdery mildew infection.

uvariifolium
H3-4 Medium-Tall *E-EM*

Pale pink flowers, usually with reddish spotting and/or a blotch in the throat. Pale indumentum on the leaf underside. Foliage is usually handsome. *R. fulvum* is closely related, smaller in all parts, with pink flowers and leaves with a reddish-brown indumentum on the underside.

wardii
H3-5 Low-Medium *M-L*

Named after the plant collector Frank Kingdon Ward, this is one of the finest yellow-flowered species and it is the parent of most of the larger yellow hybrids. Pure yellow flowers, sometimes blotched or spotted red. Oval leaves. The Himalayan *R. campylocarpum* is closely related and tends to have paler yellow flowers.

yunnanense
H3-4 Medium-Tall *M-ML*

One of the spectacular sights of Yunnan province of China are the hillsides covered in this very free-flowering, small-leaved species with pink or white flowers. Young plants are vulnerable to bark split. *R. davidsonianum* is very similar, while *R. oreotrephes* differs in its lower stature, glaucous leaves and usually purple-lavender flowers.

Larger Hybrids

These range from the ironclads, the toughest rhododendrons, bred for extremes of cold and often of heat also, to varieties suitable for woodland conditions in moderate climates. Most will start flowering at a relatively young age and flower reliably every year. In most cases the foliage is not as interesting or showy as that of the larger species listed above. Literally thousands of larger hybrids have been named and more are launched every year. Almost all the ones listed here are tried and tested and have been found reliable. One or two promising newcomers are also included. Listen to local advice as to which will grow best in your area, especially if your climate includes extremes of heat and/or cold. Most garden centers carry a range of hardy hybrids; these are not always well chosen for your area so take care!

"Britannia" is a popular old hybrid with pale red flowers and yellow looking foliage.

"Anah Kruschke"
H5-6 Medium-Tall *ML-L*

Full trusses of reddish-purple flowers on a very vigorous plant with dark foliage. Heat and sun tolerant. Not a popular color in the U.K. but a good seller in the southeastern U.S.A.

"Blue Peter"
H5 Medium *M-ML*

Frilly pale lavender-blue flowers with a prominent reddish-purple flare in the throat. Rather untidy grower that is tough and easy to please. "Blue Ensign" is similar. "A Bedford" (H5) is an upright, leggy grower with fine, pale lavender-mauve flowers with a dark flare. Useful for its heat and sun tolerance.

"Britannia"
H4 Low-Medium *ML*

This old hybrid has long been popular, but I feel it has had its day. Rather pale red flowers with foliage that tends to look yellow, however well you treat it.

"Cadis"
H5-6 Medium *ML-L*

This hybrid, with ruffled, light pink, scented flowers, is popular in the southeastern U.S.A. as it is heat tolerant and resistant to root rot. Narrow leaves give the plant a distinctive appearance. "Caroline," one of Cadis' parents, is equally heat tolerant and root-rot resistant. Lightly scented, pale pink flowers.

"Catawbiense Album"
H7 Medium-Tall *ML*

The toughest of the white, old ironclad hybrids, this is very widely grown in severest climates. Pure white flowers with a yellow-green flare. Sun, heat and wind-tolerant but takes a few years to flower freely. "Boule de Neige" is equally hardy with pure white flowers with light green/ yellow spotting. Very popular in the northeastern U.S.A. and eastern Canada. "County of York" (syn. "Catalode") (H5-6) is a very vigorous hybrid with large trusses of white with a green throat. Sun and wind tolerant.

"Christmas Cheer"
H5 Low-Medium *E-EM*

One of the best early flowering hybrids, though it only flowers at Christmas if it is forced inside. Full trusses of pink flowers gradually fade to cream. Trusses open over a long period of time, so even if some are frosted, there are usually more to come out. A dense and tidy grower and a first class plant.

"Crest"
H4 Tall *M-ML*

Among the yellow-flowered hybrids, the flowers of "Crest" have few equals, as they are large and pure yellow. The plant is upright and can look sparse. As with most yellows, it needs good drainage and is prone to mildew.

"Cunningham's White"
H5-6 Low-Medium M-ML

This very old hybrid from Cunningham's nursery in Edinburgh is one of the most widely grown throughout the world, due to its tolerance of poor or near-neutral soil, and its adaptability to full exposure. White flowers with a yellow throat. There are several clones in commerce. The most showy one has full trusses. The toughest and easiest clones have small, rather loose trusses. Used extensively as a rootstock for grafting. Good as a windbreak or screen.

"Cynthia"
H5-6 Tall ML-L

Another old favorite, this has large trusses of deep rose-pink with deeper crimson staining. Very tough: tolerant of sun and wind, and very free-flowering once it gets established.

"Erato"
H5-6 Medium ML-L

Very fine, pure red flowers in a full truss. A promising new hardy hybrid from Hachmann in Germany. "Torero" is a very similar sister seedling.

Fabia Group
H3-4 Medium ML-L

There are several clones of this woodland hybrid with pendulous flowers in loose trusses of orange or salmon pink. Leaves have a light covering of indumentum on the lower surface. Tends to grow late, so best with some shelter. "Medusa" has smaller, but more reddish-orange flowers.

Above: "Hotei," named after a Japanese deity, is one of the deepest yellow hybrids. It takes a number of years to flower and needs perfect drainage.

"Fastuosum Flore Pleno"
H5-6 Tall L

This is one of the few double-flowered hybrids. Pale bluish-mauve double-flowers (where the stamens have fused to form extra petals). A very tough and easy plant if fairly upright but tidy habit which is sun and wind tolerant.

"Golden Star"
H5 Tall M-ML

One of the best yellow hybrids for milder parts of the eastern seaboard of the northeastern U.S.A., this hybrid has large trusses of pale yellow flowers. Very vigorous and rather prone to powdery mildew. Much used as a parent for hardy yellows.

"Goldflimmer"
H5-6 Low-Medium L

One of the few rhododendrons with variegated foliage, this has flecks of yellow in the leaves. Small trusses of purplish-pink flowers. R. ponticum "Variegatum" has similar flowers while the narrow leaves have white variegation at the margins. "President Roosevelt" (H4) has red and white flowers and bold variegation in the leaves, but it sprawls and the branches are brittle.

"Goldkrone"
H5 Low-Medium *M*

This hybrid has fine yellow flowers with reddish spotting on a fairly compact plant. It requires very good drainage and is better grafted in areas with hot summers. Very free-flowering.

"Gomer Waterer"
H5-6 Medium *L*

An outstanding, reliable and very tough hybrid that is sun, heat, and wind-tolerant. White flowers, flushed lilac-pink at the edges, with a large yellowish flare. Free-flowering and useful for its late flowering time.

"Hotei"
H4 Medium *M-ML*

Named after a Japanese deity, this is one of the deepest yellow hybrids but it takes a few years to flower freely and it needs particularly good drainage.

"(The Hon. Jean) Marie de Montague"
H4 Medium *M-ML*

This has long been the standard red hybrid in the Pacific Northwest of North America. Fine crimson-scarlet flowers on a fairly upright plant. Free-flowering and useful for its sun and heat resistance.

Right: "Lady Chamberlain" is a favorite of all who see it, but it is particularly prone to powdery mildew.

Below: "(The Hon.) Jean Marie de Montague" is one of the most popular of the old red hybrids and is a big favorite in western North America.

"Lady Chamberlain"
H3-(4) Medium *M*

One of the most striking of all hybrids, this *R. cinnabarinum* hybrid has pendulous salmon-orange flowers on an upright plant with small leaves. Unfortunately this hybrid is extremely susceptible to powdery mildew as is its close relative "Lady Rosebery," which has pink flowers. Other *R. cinnabarinum* hybrids (all less susceptible to mildew) are "Biskra" (H4-5) with vermillion flowers, "Alison Johnstone" (H4) with peachy-apricot flowers, and "Conroy" (H4) with bluish leaves and light orange and rose flowers.

"Lady Clementine Mitford"
H4 Medium-Tall *ML-L*

An old hybrid, still popular, with pink flowers fading toward the center, with spotting, in a compact, rounded truss. New growth silvery. Heat and sun tolerant.

"Lem's Cameo"
H4 Medium *M-ML*

This extraordinary hybrid has revolutionized breeding and its many offspring are becoming increasingly popular in milder areas (see under "Nancy Evans"). Frilly pink cream and apricot flowers with a red blotch in the base, in huge wide trusses. Rather sparsely clothed with leaves and reluctant to branch. Bronzy new growth. Free-flowering.

"Lem's Monarch"
H4 Tall *ML*

The hybrid for the large-is beautiful brigade, this has trusses up to 12 in. (30cm) high, pale pink fading to white with a deeper rim around each flower. The extra thick foliage and stems allow the trusses to be held up well. A stunning hybrid that needs plenty of room. "Point Defiance" is very similar.

"Loderi"
H3-4 Tall *M*

The "Loderi" grex or group is a range of sister seedlings renowned for their strongly sweet-scented flowers. Huge loose trusses of pale pink to white flowers. Long pale green leaves. For best results, wind shelter and filtered shade is advisable. The most popular clones are: "King George" with white flowers, "Venus" and "Game Chick" with pale pink ones.

Above: "Lem's Monarch."

Right: "Mrs. A.T. de La Mare" is a reliable old hybrid with fine scented white flowers.

Opposite: Bred in the Pacific Northwest of the U.S.A., the cream, pink, and red flower combination and the frilled margins of the corolla have attracted many to "Lem's Cameo."

"Lord Roberts"
H5-6 Medium *L*

A useful, very tough, late flowering hybrid with small trusses of dark crimson with a black flare.

"Madame Mason"
H5-6 Low-Medium *M*

Small, compact trusses of white flowers with a yellow blotch on a dense, spreading grower. Good in southeastern U.S.A.

"Markeeta's Prize"
H4 Medium-Tall *M*

Huge, densely textured trusses of bright red flowers on a vigorous but tidy plant with thick leaves. "Halfdan Lem" is similar but with a more untidy habit.

"Mrs. A.T. de la Mare"
H5-6 Medium-Tall *M-ML*

This is one of the toughest scented hybrids. Lightly perfumed white flowers. Best in some shade to protect the flowers from the elements.

"Mrs. G.W. Leak"
H4 Medium-Tall EM-M

Rose-pink flowers, with a heavy brown and crimson flare in a full, conical truss. Upright in habit. The plant tends to suffer from leaf spot. There are many hybrids with similar pink flowers with a deeper blotch. Some of the most popular include "Mrs. Furnival," (H5-6) sun and heat-tolerant; "Furnivall's Daughter" with a larger truss and round-ended, yellowish leaves; and "Trail Blazer" (H5), recently introduced with fine pink flowers and a compact habit.

"Mrs. T. H. Lowinsky"
H5-6 Medium L

Mauve buds open to off-white flowers with a bold orange-brown flare. Vigorous and tough and useful for its late flowering. Heat-tolerant.

"Nancy Evans"
H3-4 Low-Medium M

The most popular of the many "Lem's Cameo" hybrids now coming onto the market, this is an outstanding plant with very freely-produced rounded trusses of deep yellow flowers, marked orange as they first open. Fairly compact with bronzy new growth. Needs good drainage and a little shelter for best results. There are many new hybrids with multicolored trusses coming onto the market. Time will tell which the best ones are. Some of these include the pale yellow "Horizon Monarch" and the yellow and pink "Horizon Lakeside."

Naomi Group
H4-5 Medium-Tall M-ML

There are several named clones of this cross. The most popular is "Naomi Exbury," which has rounded trusses of white to yellow flowers, with a lilac-pink edging. Subject to powdery mildew.

The deep yellow "Nancy Evans" is extremely free-flowering and is becoming popular as a garden plant in moderate areas.

Nobleanum Group
H4 Medium VE

This group of hybrids are grown for their very early flowers, opening around or before Christmas in mild winters. Small trusses of scarlet-pink, pink, or white flowers, depending on the clone. Pale green leaves have a thin layer of indumentum beneath. Habit is fairly compact but often rather irregular.

"Nova Zembla"
H6-7 Medium M

Long the standard ironclad red hybrid, this has slightly bluish-tinged red flowers on a well-behaved plant. Not worth growing in milder areas where better colors are available. Sun and fairly heat-tolerant as long as drainage is good. "America" is equally hardy, with a more spreading habit. Flowers are a rather harsh red.

"Odee Wright"
H4 **Low-Medium** *M*

Very fine trusses of pale yellow flowers with pink edging and on the reverse. Fairly compact and rather slow-growing.

"Pink Pearl"
H4 **Tall** *ML-L*

Long the standard, large pink hybrid for moderate climates, this upright grower with pale green leaves has tall pink trusses that fade out to off white. Two very similar hybrids are "Betty Wormald" with deeper pink flowers and "Marinus Koster" which is slightly more compact, as is the popular "Trude Webster."

Polar Bear Group
H3-4 **Tall** *VL*

One of the latest of the larger hybrids to flower, this large grower has fine trusses of scented white flowers, which open in July or August. Best in light shade with shelter from wind and early autumn frosts that can damage the typically late growth.

"Purple Splendor"
H4-5 **Medium** *ML*

Deep purple, frilly flowers with an almost black blotch in full trusses. The plant itself is rather lacking in vigor and is prone to powdery mildew. It being gradually superseded by its hardier and more disease-resistant offspring such as "Azurro" and "Jonathan Shaw," which have almost as deep flowers.

"Naomi Exbury" is one of the best-known Rothschild hybrids from Exbury Gardens in England.

"Roseum Elegans"
H7 **Tall** *ML*

One of the toughest and most reliable hybrids due to its hardiness and heat and sun tolerance. Rosy-lilac flowers in small trusses on a vigorous plant. Not worth growing in milder areas, but an essential plant for severest climates of rhododendron-growing areas. "English Roseum" is similar with pinker flowers, while "Catawbiense Boursault" has purple flowers.

"Rubicon" Group
H3 **Low** *M*

One of the finest low reds ever raised, but only suitable for mild areas. Very fine trusses of bright red flowers. Handsome ribbed foliage on a compact plant. Heat-tolerant. Its parent "Noyo Brave" is taller growing with paler, pinkish-red flowers. Also good in warm climates.

"Sappho"
H5-6 Medium-Tall ML-L

This old hardy hybrid has very striking white flowers with a bold, reddish-purple flair, but its deplorable straggly habit means that it should be sited at the back of a planting. Several newer hybrids such as "Calsap" have similar flowers, but an improved habit.

"Scintillation"
H5-6 Medium M-ML

This hybrid consistently wins polls in Eastern North America as the most reliable hybrid in cold, but not the coldest, areas. Rounded trusses of pink flowers with a brown flare on a plant with a tidy habit and deep green leaves. Heat-tolerant but foliage can suffer sun burn in full-exposure. "Janet Blair" (H5-6) has light pink flowers with a yellow-green flare. Free-flowering and heat-tolerant. "Brown Eyes" (H6-7) has showy bright pink flowers with a large brown flare in the throat. Rather unattractive, twisted leaves.

"September Song"
H3-4 Medium M-ML

This is one of the finest orange-flowered hybrids we have seen. The flowers are a mixture of salmon and orange. Not all that bud hardy, but free flowering otherwise. There are several new orange hybrids coming onto the market. "Mavis Davis" is one of the most promising.

"Sonata"
H4-5 Low-Medium ML-L

Small trusses of orange flowers with red centers. A compact, dense grower that is quite easy to please, as long as drainage is good. Quite free flowering once established.

"Susan"
H4-5 Medium M

A popular hybrid with fine bluish-mauve flowers in rounded trusses. Dark foliage on a fairly compact bush. Somewhat hardier are "Lavender Girl" (H5) with lightly scented pale lavender flowers and "Lavender Queen" (H5) with small rounded trusses of frilly, lavender flowers. "Mrs. Charles Pearson" (H4-5) has fine trusses of pale pinkish-mauve.

"Scintillation" consistently comes at the top of polls as the best larger hybrid for northeastern U.S.A. and eastern Canada. Well worth growing in other areas too.

"Unique"
H4 Low-Medium EM-M

Consistently one of the most popular hybrids for its tight, dense habit, this old favorite has creamy-ivory flowers flushed pink and yellow. Seems to have some heat tolerance. Best in plenty of light for best habit. "Bruce Brechtbill" is a sport of "Unique," identical in foliage but with pale pink flowers. Very popular in areas of moderate climate.

"Vanessa Pastel"
H3-4 Low ML

One of the most attractive hybrids for mild areas, this has loose trusses that open salmon-pink and fade to cream, with a red blotch in the throat. Pale green leaves on plant of quite good habit that needs protection for its late growth. Somewhat prone to powdery mildew.

"Virginia Richards" Group
H4 Medium-Tall EM

Large trusses of bright pink flowers that fade to cream, with a red center. Dark green leaves on a plant of good habit. Unfortunately this hybrid is very prone to powdery mildew, which has decreased its popularity.

"Vulcan"
H5 Medium L

Brightest red flowers on a vigorous plant, which should be in plenty of light for best habit. Shows good heat and sun tolerance but tends to produce rather yellowish late growth in the U.K. Very popular in North America.

Yellow Hammer Group
H4 Medium EM-M

This vigorous, upright hybrid has tiny leaves and masses of tubular yellow flowers from multiple buds up the stems. Needs a bit of pruning for best habit. It tends to flower quite well in autumn, as well as spring.

Deciduous Azaleas

Hybridized throughout the last 200 years, these now come in a huge variety of colors. Some flower on the bare branches while others start to shoot as the flowers open. Most are very strong, and some such as the Northern Lights series are among the toughest plants in the genus. Often used for mass planting, in woodland or in borders, the hybrids have among the brightest flowers of all rhododendrons. Many varieties are scented and some have fine autumn color. As most are relatively late-flowering, they seldom lose their flowers to spring frosts. Some of the white and yellow species and their offspring are subject to azalea powdery mildew (see page 66).

R. occidentale hybrid "Exquisita" is grown for its pastel-colored, sweetly scented flowers, which open in early June.

SPECIES

The species deciduous azaleas are becoming increasingly popular as garden plants; they are usually less flamboyant than their hybrid offspring, but with more character and often have features such as strong scent and fine autumn color. They vary considerably in hardiness.

albrechtii
H5-6 Low-Medium EM-M

Brightest rose to deep rose-purple flowers on the bare stems. Although hardy, the rather early flowers and growth need some shelter.

arborescens
H5 Low-Medium ML-L

A fine, compact species with scented white to pale pink flowers with long red stamens and style. There are many Eastern American scented species of similar appearance: *atlanticum* (H5-6) has glaucous leaves and a low, spreading habit; *prinophyllum* (H7) has scented, pink flowers; *viscosum* (H5-6)

has very late small white flowers; *canescens* with pale to deep pink flowers is suitable for milder areas with hot summers only.

calendulaceum
H7 Medium-Tall L

This species is the source of much of the bright orange color in the hybrids. Small, bright yellow or orange flowers. *cumberlandense* (H5-6) is very similar, with fine red forms; *prunifolium* (H5-6) with orange-red to vivid red flowers is late flowering and very heat tolerant; *austrinum* (H3-4) with yellow or orange yellow flowers is less hardy but very heat-tolerant. Good in its native southeastern U.S.A.

luteum
H5 Medium-Tall ML-L

This is the vigorous Pontic azalea, widely planted in the U.K. and elsewhere for its fine, sweetly scented, yellow flowers and its very good autumn colors.

molle ssp. japonicum (syn. Azalea mollis)
H7 Low-Medium M-ML

Red, orange, salmon, pink, or yellow flowers. Very tough and easy. Widely grown under the name *Azalea mollis*.

occidentale
H4-5 Medium-Tall L-VL

The western American native azalea with large, sweetly-scented, white

flowers, usually flushed pink, with a yellow flare, in quite large trusses. Not as hardy as most of the other species and subject to azalea powdery mildew and rust.

schlippenbachii
H7 Low-Medium EM

Very showy pink or white flowers on a compact plant with distinctive leaves. Although midwinter hardy, its flowers and new growth are vulnerable to spring frost damage.

vaseyi
H5-6 Medium EM-M

A very distinctive azalea with attractive two-lipped, pink or white flowers on a bushy plant. Pointed leaves show good autumn color.

HYBRIDS

The following are the most commonly grown named varieties in the various hybrid groups. Some, such as Mollis and Exbury, are often sold as seedlings to color, rather than as named varieties.

Ghent
H6-7 **Medium-Tall**
M-ML

The oldest hybrid group, this contains tough, usually small-flowered cultivars, including the currently fashionable small, double-flowered varieties. The most commonly sold varieties are:
"Coccinea Speciosa" Orange-red with yellow, single.
"Daviesii" White and yellow (two clones-one single and one double).
"Narcissiflora" Double pale yellow.

Mollis
H6-7 **Low-Medium**
M-ML

The earliest-flowering azalea group, these are mostly not hybrids but simply selections of the Japanese species *R. molle* ssp. *japonicum*. Colors range from red to orange, salmon, pink, and yellow. More compact and spreading than the other hybrid groups. Most often sold as seedlings to color. The most common named clones are:
"Adriaan Koster" pure yellow.
"Christopher Wren" yellow, with orange flare.
"Dr. M. Oosthoek" vivid orange-red.
"Koster's Brilliant Red" reddish-orange.
"Lemonora" yellow, shaded pink.

The white seedling Knaphill or Exbury azalea, suitable for extreme climates. This group of azaleas are available in a variety of colors from white to yellow, salmon, pink, orange, and red.

Exbury/Knaphill
H5-H7 **Medium-Tall**
ML-L

The most flamboyant of all the hybrid groups and containing the largest number of cultivars. Development of these hybrids began at Knaphill nursery and continued at Exbury (both in England). Subsequent work has followed in several parts of the world, including Ilam in New Zealand and Arensons and Girards in the U.S.A. Some varieties are scented. There are far too many named hybrids. Some of the most popular include:

"Balzac" Large trusses of orange-red flowers.
"Berryrose" Pale pink with orange, fragrant. Bronzy new growth.
"Cannon's Double" Double pink with orange shading.
"Cecile" Salmon pink with a yellow blotch.
"Chetco" Yellow with an orange blotch.
"Fireball" Deep orange-red.
"George Reynolds" Large, deep yellow flowers, orange spotting.
"Gibraltar" The most popular orange-flowered selection.

"**Glowing Embers**" Orange-red with an orange flare. Compact.

"**Golden Sunset**" Light yellow, tinged orange, orange flare.

"**Homebush**" Double pink flowers in rounded, balled truss.

"**Hotspur**" Reddish-orange flowers.

"**Klondyke**" One of the best yellows. New-growth coppery-red.

"**Mount Saint Helens**" Yellowish-pink with an orange flare, fragrant.

"**Oxydol**" Large white flowers with a yellow throat.

"**Persil**" Pure white with a deep yellow flare.

"**Royal Lodge**" Deep red with long, protruding stamens.

"**Satan**" Not surprisingly, this is deep reddish-orange.

"**Silver Slipper**" White, edged pink, with yellow flare.

"**Strawberry Ice**" Pink with a yellow blotch.

"**Syliphides**" Light pink, with yellow shadings.

"**Whitethroat**" Masses of smallish, scented white flower.

Northern Lights Azaleas
H7 or colder Medium-Tall ML-L

Bred for severest climates, the Northern Lights series are hardy to -40°F (-34°C)

Above: "Irene Koster" is one of the most popular of the *R. occidentale* hybrid deciduous azaleas, with its fine, scented pink and white flowers.

Left: "Golden Sunset," a fine yellow Exbury azalea, which flowers in late May and early June.

and are amongst the hardiest plants in the genus. They have small flowers and are probably not worth growing in milder climates where less hardy varieties are suitable.

"**Golden Lights**" yellow, fragrant.

"**Lemon Lights**" Bright yellow.

"**Mandarin Lights**" Ruffled light orange flowers, light fragrance.

"**Northern Hi-Lights**" White with a yellow blotch, mildew resistant.

"**Orchid Lights**" Lilac flowers, low and bushy.

"**Rosy Lights**" Pink with deeper shadings; fragrant.

"**Spicy Lights**" Tangerine-orange, fragrant.

"**White Lights**" White, quite large flowers, fragrant.

occidentale
H4-5 Low-Medium ML-L

Bred from the species *R. occidentale*, these hybrids have pale-colored flowers and most are scented. As the least hardy group, most are suitable for moderate climates only. Many are susceptible to azalea mildew.

"**Delicatissima**" White, flushed yellow and pink, blotched yellow, scented.

"**Exquisita**" White, flushed pink, orange blotch, scented.

"**Irene Koster**" Pale pink, fading to cream, deeper stripes, scented.

"**Washington State Centennial**" (syn. "Centennial") White with huge yellow blotch.

Evergreen or Japanese Azaleas

Worldwide, these are the most popular members of the genus, making fine houseplants as well as garden plants, thriving in climates too hot or dry for other rhododendrons. The selection and breeding of azaleas goes back hundreds of years in Japan and hybridization began here in the West as soon as many of the varieties were introduced, mostly in the early 1900s. Many evergreen azaleas are cold and heat-tolerant but are not successful in northern climates, where summers are not hot enough to ripen the wood. A number of the varieties that grow well elsewhere are not good performers in Scotland, Germany, Scandinavia, and eastern Canada, for instance, and breeders in these areas have produced hybrids to suit these climates. Evergreen azaleas are subject to azalea gall and petal blight (see page 70).

The various breeding programs divide the varieties into categories such as Satsuki, Kurume and Glendale. Varieties with double flowers have fused stamens, giving a ruffled effect in the center of the flower. Varieties described as "hose-in-hose" have two rings of petals, one inside the other.

The various cultivar groups are listed in order of hardiness, with the tender ones listed first. Flowering times are hard to tie down, as in very mild climates, many will flower in winter and early spring, while in cold climates the same varieties may not flower till late spring.

A double flowered Indica azalea that can be grown outdoors in mild areas and a popular houseplant in colder regions.

Satsuki and Gumpo
H3 ML-L

The Japanese have been selecting and naming these spectacular azaleas for hundreds of years. Many of them have different colors of flowers on one plant with dots, spots, rings, and other effects. This makes naming some of them a nightmare and a bit meaningless as you never know what color you will get next. Most of the ones listed below are stable as far as flower color is concerned. Best in partial shade to allow flowers to last. Very popular as potted plants and for bonsai. Very poor in areas without summer heat to ripen the wood.
"Flame Creeper" Single orange-red. Low, spreading habit.
"Gumpo" Large single white, low, dense.
"Gumpo Pink" Single rose-pink flowers with deep flecks, low and dense.
"Higasa" Large single deep rose-pink flowers.
"Shinnyo No Tsuki" Large white with pink flecks.

Kurume
H3-4 EM-M

These compact plants, first imported from Japan to the west by E. Wilson (as the Wilson 50), have masses of small flowers. Further hybrids were made of them in many parts of the world. Best in part shade in warmer and more southern climates. Most are not reliable in northern climates; the hardier ones are noted.
"Addy Wery" Strong red, upright habit. Fairly hardy.
"Amoenum" Hose-in-hose, rosy-purple, low and spreading.
"Blauu's Pink" (M) Yellowish-pink, hose-in-hose, with a dark blotch.
"Coral Bells" Small, hose-in-hose, pink with darker centers. Small leaves.
"Hexe" Crimson hose-in-hose on a low spreader.
"Hino Crimson" Small, bright red flowers. Red winter foliage.
"Hinodegiri" (M) Small flowered, purplish-red. Quite hardy.
"Kirin" Hose-in-hose, two-tone pink. Good in southern England.
"Mother's Day" (L) Bright red, semi-double. Quite hardy.
"Mucronatum" Upright habit with large white flowers.

Gable, Kaempferi, and Vuykiana
H4-(5/6)

This group contains many of the taller-growing and large-flowered hybrids raised from the species *R. kaempferi* and *R. poukhanense*. Many of the hybrids have inherited their parents' semi-deciduous nature and they can look rather sparse in winter. Many of them benefit from hardy pruning, especially when young. Many are suitable for colder climates such as Scotland and varieties such as "Johanna" are among the most popular evergreen azaleas in Europe.

kaempferi (H3-5 M-L) This very variable Japanese species has reddish, orange-red, salmon pink, pink or, rarely, white flowers. Rather a rangy grower which tends to be semi-deciduous.

poukhanense. (syn. *yedoense* var. *poukhanense*) (H5-6 M) This Korean species is one of the toughest evergreen azalea species, and has been a very important parent of the some of the hardiest hybrids. Rose to pale lilac-purple flowers.

"**Blue Danube**" (M-ML) Fine deep purplish-red. Vigorous. Popular in U.K.

"**Caroline Gable**" (ML) Red, hose-in-hose, medium-tall.

"**Fedora**" (M) Deep-rose to salmon pink, single.

"**Hardy Gardenia**" ("Linwood") Double white, good foliage.

"**Johanna**" Carmine-red. Fine dark glossy foliage. Very popular.

"**Palestrina**" (H6) Large white flowers. Erect habit. One of the hardiest.

"**Purple Splendor**" (M-ML) Reddish-purple, frilled. Fairly compact.

"**Rosebud**" (ML) Double pink, like miniature rosebuds. Compact.

"**Rose Greeley**" (M-ML) Hose-in-hose, white with greenish-yellow blotch.

"**Orange Beauty**" (M) Salmon-orange, tall, semi-deciduous.

The double-pink evergreen azalea "Rosebud" is one of the most popular in many parts of the world.

"**Stewartsontonian**" (H6 M) Large, single, bright red. Red winter foliage.

"**White Rosebud**" Double white, dense upright habit.

"**Vuyk's Scarlet**" (ML) Very popular in U.K. Large scarlet flowers.

Eastern American Hybrids, Glenn Dale, Etc.
H4-5

The Glenn Dales, bred by Ben Morrison in Maryland, includes crosses made with many of the varieties previously mentioned. The hardiest ones are suitable for much of coastal northeastern U.S.A and they are very popular in the Pacific Northwest. A few are popular in Europe. Most not reliably hardy in Scotland.

"Buccaneer" (M) Large, brilliant orange-red. Upright. Needs shade.
"Chippewa" (VL) Late-flowering frilled bright pink. Compact. Hardy.
"Everest" (M-ML) One of the finest large-flowered, compact whites.
"Glacier" (M) single white, glossy leaves.
"Glamour" (M) Single bright rose-red. Bronze winter foliage.
"Martha Hitchcock" (ML) Very showy, white with reddish-purple margins.
"Megan" (L) Large purplish pink flowers. Needs pruning.

Eastern American Hardiest Hybrids
H5-6

This category includes the hardiest azaleas, suitable for extreme climates. Some of these have proven not to be hardy in milder, northern areas, due to lack of summer heat. This group includes varieties bred by Robin Hill, Shamarello.

"Cascade" (H6 M-ML) White.
"Elsie Lee" (H6 M-ML) An upright grower with double lavender flowers. Good in U.K.

"Megan" is one of the most popular of the Glenn Dale azaleas from eastern U.S.A. Very showy, large purple flowers on a rather rangy bush which needs pruning when young.

"Girard's Hotshot"(syn. "Hotshot") (H5-6 M) Single red, good foliage.
"Helen Curtis" (H6-7) Double-white flowers, spreading habit. Very hardy.
"Hino Red" (H6-7 M) Red, spreading but compact.
"Nancy of Robin Hill" (H4-5) Hose-in-hose, semi-double pink. Low-growing.
"Red Red" (H6 M) Very fine red flowers. Not reliable in Scotland.

Kiusianum and Nakaharae & Their Hybrids
H4-6

The dwarf species *R. kiusianum* and *R. nakaharae* have been crossed with larger-flowered but less hardy varieties to create selections satisfactory for Scotland, Scandinavia, Germany, eastern Canada, and other similar climates where summer sun strength is not reliable. The most important hybridizers are Polly Hill (U.S.A.), Peter Cox (Scotland), and G. Ahrends, C. Fleischmann and H. Hachmann (Germany). Most are low-growing, tolerant of full exposure and fairly evergreen.

Kiusianum (H5 M-L Dwarf). This deciduous, or semideciduous, species has tiny leaves and is usually slow-growing and compact. The masses of small flowers can be white, pink, purple, red, or orange-red. Much used in hybridizing.
nakaraharae (H5-(6) L-VL Dwarf). This Taiwanese species is useful for its low, creeping, or spreading habit and its late flowers which range from salmon to orange-red and red. Very slow-growing and compact. "Mt. Seven Star" is perhaps the best clone.
"Alexander" (H5-6 L) Deep reddish-orange with deep blotch, creeping habit.
"Canzonetta" (H5-6) Hose-in-hose, brightest pink. Compact. Good In northern Europe.

"Squirrel" (H5 L) Masses of small scarlet flowers, good foliage. Good in Scotland.
"Susannah Hill" (H5 L) Strong red with deeper spotting, low and spreading.
"Wombat" (H5 ML-L) Bright pink flowers on a low, carpeting plant. Good in U.K.

"Diamant" (H5-6) A range of *R. kiusianum* hybrids in colors ranging from purple, red, pink, to white. Compact and dense with small leaves and masses of small flowers. Very tough, and excellent in northern Europe.
"Geisha Orange" (H5 M) Salmon-orange, small flowered, compact, and low.

"Kermesina" (H5-6 ML) A compact, small-leaved and small-flowered azalea popular in Europe. Bright pink flowers. "Kermesina Rose" is a sport of the above with pink flowers, edged white. Very distinctive. "Kermesina White" is a white form of the above.
"Panda" (H5 ML) Compact with fine white flowers. Very popular in U.K.
"Pink Pancake" (H5 L) Low carpeter with single pink flowers. There are many similar selections from the same breeder.

Above:
R. kiusianum is a fine plant for the rock garden.

Right:
"Canzonetta" is a tough, recently named German evergreen azalea with double flowers of very bright pink and a low compact habit.

Opposite:
The sport "Kermesina Rose" is a very popular, low-growing evergreen azalea, ideal for northern. climates.

Tender Rhododendrons

These fall into two categories: those which can take a limited amount of frost (temperate species) and those which must be kept more or less frost-free (Vireyas).

TEMPERATE SPECIES AND HYBRIDS

These species and their hybrids vary in hardiness from H3 to H1 and in mild climates such as the western seaboard of the U.K., and Ireland, parts of France and Italy, California, and Vancouver Island, most of New Zealand and parts of southern Australia, they make superb garden plants, producing compact, free-flowering specimens with flowers ranging from lavender and pink though white to yellow. In colder climates, they make excellent indoor plants for the greenhouse. Many of the plants listed below are scented. All appreciate good drainage and an open compost. (See pages 40-41 for more details.) Unless you live in a mild climate, these varieties are likely only to be available from specialty nurseries.

burmanicum
H2-3 Low EM-M

The plant usually grown under the name *R. burmanicum* is actually a hybrid and is one of the best yellow hybrids for warm climates. Masses of yellow flowers on a fairly tidy plant with scaly leaves. There are many fine hybrids of this plant, such as "Saffron Queen" and "Owen Pearce," which are similar in flower and habit.

edgeworthii
H2-3 Low-Medium EM-M

For both flowers and foliage, this is one of the finest choices. Usually sweetly scented, white or white-flushed-pink flowers in trusses of three. Deep green leaves have a distinctive rough upper surface

and the lower surface is covered with a layer of brown indumentum. Needs exceptionally good drainage, and good out outdoors in an old tree-stump or similar. Variable in hardiness; the hardiest forms are worth trying in a sheltered spot, even in climates such as eastern Scotland.

formosum
H2-3 Medium EM-L

A variable species in foliage, flowers and hardiness. Var. *formosum* tends to be hardier, usually having scented flowers, white, sometimes blotched yellow, flushed pink. The more tender Var. *inaequale* has perhaps the strongest scent of the Maddenia species. Flowers white with a yellow blotch.

"Fragrantissimum"
H2 Medium ML-L

One of the most widely-grown hybrids of this type. White, pink-tinged flowers have a yellow throat and a fine nutmeg-like sweet scent. Very straggly, putting out long shoots that can be trained around stakes or trellis. Subject to rust and mildew. "Lady Alice Fitzwilliam" has a less powerful scent, but is much more compact, making a better indoor plant.

"Else Frye" from California has fine scented flowers, white, slightly flushed pink and yellow.

lindleyi
H2-3 Medium EM-M

Magnificent fragrant trumpets, up to 4 in. (10cm) long, in trusses of three to seven, are usually white with pink flushing. A rather ungainly, straggly grower best grown as an informal thicket, allowing the long shoots to scramble about. Rather too big and untidy for pot culture. Hardiest forms (often Ludlow and Sherriff collections) are worth trying outdoors in climates such as eastern Scotland in a favorable site. *R. dalhousiae* (H2) has creamy yellow flowers while *R. dalhousiae* Var. *rhabdotum* (H1-2) has an extraordinary red stripe down the side of the corolla. *R. veitchianum* (H1-2) is variable in flower but usually has frilled white flowers, sometimes scented. Cubittii Group has fine white flowers, flushed pink, with a yellow-orange flare.

moulmainense
H1-2 Low-Tall *E-M*

This little-known species has huge potential as a garden plant in mild and hot areas such as California and New Zealand. Plentiful white, pink, or violet flowers can produce a spectacular effect on a mature plant. Flowers are generally scented. It usually has a showy reddish-purple, smooth, or peeling bark. This species is sometimes grown under names such as *R. ellipticum*. There are other equally fine, closely related species such as *R. stamineum* with tubular white flowers.

nuttallii
H1-2 Tall *E-M*

This species has among the largest individual flowers in the genus *Rhododendron*, up to 5 in. (12.5cm) long, in trusses of three to six. Flowers are white or cream, usually tinged pink and/or yellow and are strongly scented. Huge, wrinkled leaves, up to 10 in. (24cm) long, are bronzy or reddish in young growth. A vigorous, upright grower, it needs a large space to grow indoors. Very popular in very mild rhododendron-growing areas. There are many named and unnamed hybrids of this species crossed with *R. lindleyi* such as "Mi Amor" and "Tupare," which are equally finely scented and spectacular. The recently introduced species *R. excellens* also has large leaves, but its flowers are not as large as those of *R. nuttallii*.

VIREYAS

This group of rhododendrons are found on mountains in Indonesia, Papua New Guinea, Malaysia, the Philippines, and in other parts of Southeast Asia. There is one species in northern Australia. Unless you live in an area where frosts are almost unknown (Auckland, and north of it in New Zealand; Los Angeles, California; and other similar climates), you will have to grow these plants indoors, in a more or less frost-free greenhouse or conservatory. For sheer flamboyance with brightest yellows, oranges, and reds, not to mention multicolored flowers, the Vireyas have few equals, and anyone who sees them is captivated.

All are rated H0, though some varieties can take a degree or two of frost, for a short period. In the wild and outdoors, Vireyas can get to 16 ft. (5m) or more, but in cultivation, such large plants are seldom seen. Larger growers will reach 6 ft. 7 in. (2m), while some of the smaller ones scarcely reach 12 in. (30cm). As they come from near the equator, Vireyas tend not to respond to seasons and can therefore flower or grow at any time of year. There are several hundred species and many hybrids to choose from. Most are only available from specialty nurseries. The following is a small selection of some of the most commonly grown species and hybrids.

jasminiflorum

This species has tubular white (sometimes flushed pink) flowers in fine trusses. The flowers have a delicious, sweet scent. Other species with scented, tubular, white flowers include *R. tuba* and *R. suaveolens*.

javanicum

One of the finest orange-flowered (sometimes yellow) rhododendron species, which can get quite large. A parent of many hybrids such as the bright orange-pink "Souvenir De J.H. Mangles." *R. polyanthemum* from Borneo has equally spectacular trusses of orange-red.

laetum

One of the finest deep pure yellow flowers to be found in the genus. Vigorous and best with some pruning.

lochiae

The only native rhododendron to Australia, this species has bright red or deep pink flowers. "Valentine" is a popular hybrid of *R. lochiae* with masses of pendulous red flowers on a compact, small-leaved plant.

macgregoriae

Rounded trusses of up to 15 yellow orange or red flowers. Usually vigorous and fairly tidy. One of the easiest species for beginners and a parent of many hybrids such as the bright yellow "Buttermaid" and the white, scented "Scotchburn White."

nervulosum

Is a little-known species with very distinctive narrow leaves and bright scarlet or orange flowers. We find this one of the easiest species to please.

zoelleri

One of the most spectacular species with orange or red flowers with yellow centers. A vigorous, rather rangy grower.

Opposite: The vireya species *R. polyanthemum* from Borneo has fine salmon-red or orange-red flowers. Rather slow-growing, this is a species for experienced gardeners.

Right: *R. macgregoriae* is one of the easiest of the Vireya species to cultivate. The flowers are usually a mixture of yellow and orange.

Above: The magnificent Vireya species *R. zoelleri* has been used as a parent of many hybrids.

OTHER HYBRIDS

Some of the many other hybrids available include: "Annata Gold" (yellow and orange, tall), "Charming Valentino" (reddish-pink, compact habit), "Dr. Herman Sleumer" (pink, with a creamy-yellow throat, scented), "Moonwood" (ivory white, compact habit), "Ne Plus Ultra" (bright red, vigorous), "Sunny" (bright orange and yellow, vigorous), "Toff" (yellow, with salmon pink border).

Glossary,
Bibliography,
Recommended
Varieties and
Index

Glossary

axillary
(bud) coming from an axil, which is the angle between a leaf stalk and a stem. Species such as *R. racemosum* produce flowers from axillary buds.

bark split
a physical injury; the sap in the stem is frozen while the plant is in growth, causing the bark to split. It can be fatal in severe cases.

calyx, calyces
the outermost of the floral envelopes, particularly prominent in species such as *R. thomsonii*. The calyx is often significant in species identification.

chlorosis
a yellowing of the leaves caused by mineral imbalance, disease, too much or too little water, or climatic or genetic problems.

clone
a genetically uniform collection of individuals derived from a single individual by asexual vegetative propagation (i.e., not grown from seed). The finest forms of species are often given clonal names e.g., *R. calostrotum* "Gigha" F.C.C.

corolla
the tube and lobes (petals) of the flower.

elepidote
(opposite of **lepidote**) without SCALES. This distinction is of fundamental importance in the classification of rhododendrons.

epiphyte
a plant which grows on another plant (a fallen log, for example) but which does not derive any nutrients from it.

Ericaceae
the plant family that includes rhododendrons, heathers, *Kalmia*, *Gaultheria*, and several other genera. Hence, *Ericaceous*, belonging to the family Ericaceae.

felted
(indumentum) matted with intertwined hairs such as in the **indumentum** of *R. phaeochrysum* var. *phaeochrysum* and *R. sphaeroblastum*.

glabrous
without hairs or glands of any kind.

gland
a hair with a small spherical knob of sticky secretary tissue, hence glandular. Glands can be found on branchlets, leaves, and parts of the flower and are an important diagnostic tool in identifying species.

glaucous
(leaf) green, strongly tinged with bluish gray; with a grayish waxy bloom, for example in *R. campanulatum* ssp. *aeruginosum*, *R. lepidostylum*, *R. oreotrephes*.

hose-in-hose
(flower) a second COROLLA within the first.

indumentum
a covering of hairs found on leaves, which can be thick and woolly or thin. The different types are very important for species identification.

lax
(truss) one in which the flowers hang downward, often between the foliage.

lepidote
1) the scaly part of the genus *Rhododendron* in subgenus Rhododendron, the opposite of **elepidote** (without scales). This distinction is of fundamental importance in the classification of rhododendrons. 2) with **scales** on the shoots, leaves, and flower parts.

Maddenia
(subsection) This group of species are rather tender, often grown indoors, and many of them, and their hybrids, are sweetly scented.

nectar pouches or nectaries
sac-like vessels in the base of the corolla of some species of rhododendron containing a sweet substance, found in most species of Subsections Irrorata and Thomsonia, for example.

oval
(leaf) egg-shaped but more or less rounded at both ends, e.g., *R. callimorphum*.

petal blight
a fungal disease which destroys flowers, turning them brown and limp.

Phytophthora
a genus containing many serious pathogenic fungus diseases, especially rootrot, *Phytophthora cinnamoni*.

pinching
a method of preventative pruning, where the terminal bud or growth is removed, to encourage branching and a denser growth habit.

powdery mildew
a disease that attacks rhododendrons, causing leaf discoloration or leaf drop and that can be fatal in severe infections. Can be controlled with fungicides.

radiate
Spreading from a common center.

root rot (see under *Phytophthora*)

rust
a fungal disease that causes black spotting on the leaf's upper surface with corresponding reddish-brown patches of spores on the leaf's lower surface.

scales
found on the leaves of LEPIDOTE rhododendrons; these can sometimes be seen with the naked eye but are better magnified so their form can be used to aid identification.

shrub
a woody plant with several stems or branches from near the base; of smaller stature than a tree.

stamen
the male organ of the flower that bears the pollen.

stigma
the female part of the flower, at the end of the style, which is receptive to the pollen.

subsection
in the taxonomy of rhododendrons, the genus is divided up into subsections which contain 1-30 or more related species. For instance, subsection Triflora contains mostly tall and upright-growing scaly-leaved species with masses of tall flowers.

suckering
producing shoots from near or below ground level, often by rootstocks below the grafted union.

taxonomy
the science of the identification, nomenclature and classification of plants.

truss
a cluster of flowers on a single stalk.

vine weevil
a pernicious insect pest which notches foliage, and whose grubs eat roots and bark.

Vireya
part of the Genus *Rhododendron* is section Vireya which contains s everal hundred flamboyant tropical species which need frost free conditions in which to grow.

Bibliography

BEAN, W.J., *Trees and Shrubs Hardy in the British Isles*, Vol. III, 8th Revised Edition, John Murray, 1976.

CHAMBERLAIN, D.F., *Notes from the Royal Botanic Garden, Edinburgh*, Vol. 39, No. 2, Revision of Rhododendron 2, Subgenus Hymenanthes. H.M.S.O., 1982.

COX, K.N.E. *A Plantsman's Guide to Rhododendrons*, Ward Lock, 1989, 1993.

COX, P.A., *The Smaller Rhododendrons*, Batsford, 1985.

COX, P.A., *The Larger Rhododendron Species*, Batsford, 1990.

COX, P.A. *The Cultivation of Rhododendrons*, Batsford, 1993.

COX. P.A. & COX, K.N.E. *Cox's Guide to Choosing Rhododendrons*, Batsford, 1990.

COX, P.A. & COX, K.N.E. *The Encyclopedia of Rhododendron Hybrids*, Batsford, 1988.

COX, P.A. & COX, K.N.E. *The Encyclopedia of Rhododendron Species*, Glendoick Publishing, 1997.

CULLEN, J., *Notes from the Royal Botanic Garden, Edinburgh*, Vol. 39, No. 1, Revision of Rhododendron 1, Subgenus Rhododendron, sections Rhododendron & Pogonanthum. Her Majesty's Stationary Office, 1980.

DAVIDIAN, H.H., *The Rhododendron Species, Vol. I, Lepidotes*, Batsford, 1982.

DAVIDIAN, H.H., *The Rhododendron Species, Vol. II, Elepidotes, Series Arboreum to Lacteum*, Batsford, 1989.

DAVIDIAN, H.H., *The Rhododendron Species, Vol. III, Elepidotes continued*, Timber Press, 1992.

DAVIDIAN H.H., *The Rhododendron Species, Vol IV, Azaleas*, Timber Press, 1995.

GALLE, FRED C., *Azaleas*, Timber Press, 1985.

GREER H. *Greer's Guidebook to Available Rhododendrons*, Offshoot publications 1982, 1996.

KINGDON-WARD, F., *The Romance of Plant Hunting*, Arnold, 1924. + many other works.

LEACH, D.G., *Rhododendrons of the World*, Allen & Unwin, 1962.

POSTAN C. (ed.) *The Rhododendron Story*, Royal Horticultural Society, 1996.

VARIOUS *Azaleas, Rhododendrons & Camellias*, Sunset Books, 1982.

Journal of the American Rhododendron Society.

Recommended varieties

The following lists are not exhaustive and are simply to give you ideas in searching for the best varieties for any given purpose or climate.

Ironclads for extreme climates H7
minus var. *carolinianum*
"P.J.M. Group"
"Ramapo"
yakushimanum
brachycarpum
catawbiense
dauricum
"America"
"Catawbiense Album"
"Nova Zembla"
"Roseum Elegans"
"Brown Eyes"
+ many D. Leach hybrids.

azaleas:
arborescens
calendulaceum
japonicum
kiusianum
vaseyi
"Northern Lights" azaleas

Cold-hardy species H5-6
adenogynum
calophytum
degronianum
hippophaeoides
keiskei
fortunei
mucronulatum
pachysanthum
roxieanum
smirnowii

Cold hardy hybrids H5-6
"Cunningham's White"
"Cynthia"
"Fastuosum Flore Pleno"
"Goldflimmer"
"Gomer Waterer"
"Erato"
"Mrs Furnival"
"Scintilliaton"
"Taurus"

Varieties with heat tolerance
minus var. *chapmanii*
maximum
Subsection Maddenia species & hybrids.
"Anah Krushke"
"Caroline"
"Cadis"
"Lady Clementine Mitford"
"Mrs T.H. Lowinsky"
"Roseum Elegans"
"Scintilliation"
"Vulcan"

Many varieties of deciduous and evergreen azaleas.

Varieties for very mild climates H0-2
arboreum
burmanicum + hybrids
macabeanum
nuttallii
sinogrande
"Fragrantissimum"
"Mi Amor"
nuttallii
"Noyo Brave"
"Rubicon"

Indica & Satsuki azaleas
many deciduous azaleas

Vireyas (frost-free)

Best foliage
Large

falconeri
macabeanum
rex
sinogrande

Best foliage
Low-Medium

bureavii
campanulatum ssp. *aeruginosum*
elegantulum
exasperatum
orbiculare
pachysanthum

Best foliage
Semi-dwarf/dwarf.

edgeworthii
lepidostylum
pronum
proteoides
roxieanum
williamsianum
yakushimanum

Early flowering
barbatum
dauricum "Midwinter"
"Lucy Lou"
"Nobleanum"
mucronulatum
oreodoxa
"Christmas Cheer"
"Praecox"
"Ptarmigan"
"Tessa Roza" & "Bianca"

Neutral or slightly alkaline soil
decorum
hirsutum
makinoi
rubiginosum
vernicosum
"Cunningham's White"

Scented
arborescens
decorum
edgeworthii
fortunei
luteum
"Mi Amor"
occidentale
"Fragrantissimum"
"Lady Alice Fitzwilliam"
"Loderi"

Best Yak hybrids
"Caroline Allbrook"
"Dopey"
"Fantastica"
"Hydon Dawn"
"Ken Janeck"
"Mardi Gras"
"Morgenrot"
"Percy Wiseman"
"Skookum"
"Sneezy"
"Solidarity"
"Titian Beauty"

RECOMMENDED PLANTS

Easy dwarfs:

"Curlew," "Dora Amateis," *fastigiatum*, "Intrifast," *keleticum*, "Patty Bee," "Ptarmigan," "Ramapo," "Scarlet Wonder."

Easy semi-dwarfs and "Yaks":

"Elisabeth Hobbie," "Fantastica," "Linda," "Percy Wiseman," "Praecox," "Titian Beauty," "Unique," *viridescens*, "Winsome."

Easy larger species:

bureavii, dauricum, decorum, oreodoxa, rex ssp. *fictolacteum, rubiginosum, vernicosum, wardii, yunnanense.*

Easy medium sized hybrids:

"Christmas Cheer," "Cunningham's White," "Gomer Waterer," "Jean Marie de Montague," "Nancy Evans," "Scintillation."

Easy larger hybrids:

"Grace Seabrook," "Fastuosum Flore Pleno," "Markeeta"s Prize," "Taurus."

Best foliage, dwarfs:

fastigiatum, lepidostylum, yakushimanum, "Blue Silver," "Intrifast," "Ramapo," *viridescens, williamsianum.*

Best foliage, medium:

bureavii, elegantulum, insigne, pachysanthum, pseudochrysanthum, "Elizabeth Lockhart"

Best foliage, large:

falconeri, macabeanum, niveum, rex, sinogrande, "Sir Charles Lemon."

Late-flowering:

calostrotum "Nitens," *auriculatum, hemsleyanum*, "Polar Bear," *nakaharae.*

Cold sites, low-growing:

hippophaeoides, lapponicum, yakushimanum, "Arctic Tern," "P.J.M.," "Ramapo," "Scarlet Wonder."

Cold/exposed sites, large:

"Cunninghams's White," "Fastuosum Flore Pleno," "Gomer Waterer," "Mme Masson," "Azurro," "Erato," "Goldflimmer."

Best white:

decorum, yunnanense (white), "Arctic Tern," "Crane," "Cunningham"s White," "Loderi," "Lucy Lou," "Dora Amateis," "Ptarmigan," "Panda" (azalea).

Best pink:

oreodoxa, "Christmas Cheer," "Linda," "Pintail," "Fantastica," "Canzonetta" (azalea).

Best yellow:

campylocarpum, wardii, "Curlew," "Odee Wright," "Yellowhammer," "Nancy Evans," "Klondyke" (Exbury).

Best red:

"Captain Jack," *cerasinum, cinnabarinum* "Roylei," "Dopey," "Elisabeth Hobbie," "Grace Seabrook" or "Taurus," "Jean Marie de Montague," "Vulcan." Evergreen azaleas: "Squirrel," "Red Red," "Racoon."

Best blue-purple:

fastigiatum, keleticum, russatum, augustinii, "Night Sky," "Penheale Blue," "St Breward," "Azurro," "Fastuosum Flore Pleno," "Susan."

Best orange:

citriniflorum var *horaeum* (orange), *dichroanthum, cinnabarinum* "Concatenans," "Fabia," "September Song," "Sonata," "Gibraltar" (Exbury).

Conservatory:

edgeworthii, formosum var. *inequale, dalhousiae* var. *rhabdotum*, "Lady Alice Fitzwilliam."

Index